a short & happy guide to

Business Organizations

Third Edition

David G. Epstein

A SHORT & HAPPY GUIDE® SERIES

WEST ACADEMIC

860 Blue Gentian Road, Suite 350
Eagan, MN 55121
1-877-888-1330

Published in the United States of America

ISBN: 979-8-89209-994-3

Acknowledgments

I would like to acknowledge the contribution of the thousands of students from the University of North Carolina Law School, the University of Texas Law School, the University of Arkansas Law School, the Emory Law School, Southern Methodist University Law School, the North Carolina Central School of Law, and the University of Richmond Law School who took my Business Associations course (called "Business Organizations" at some of the schools and "Corporations" at some others). What they wrote and didn't write on their final exams strongly influenced what I wrote in this short and happy guide to business associations final exams.

And, I would like to acknowledge the important work of Professors Bainbridge,[1] Freer, Gevurtz, Hamilton, and Moll. Those guys obviously really know a lot about business associations. Reading their comprehensive student texts on business associations has been very helpful to me in preparing for class and could be very helpful to you.

---

[1] Okay to tell your prof that you are using student guides by Bainbridge, or Freer, or . . . Might not be a good idea to tell your prof that you are using my book. Some professors I know think that I have made Business Associations too easy.

Table of Contents

A Short & Happy Guide to Business Organizations

Third Edition

First Word: Short

The first word is "short." This book is short, It has only 235 pages. And small pages at that. With lots of space between lines

The reason that this book has only 235 small pages and other student texts on business associations have more than 600 big pages is that this book is not a student text on business associations. This book is a student text on business associations exams.[1]

My goal is not to teach you BA/BO. My more limited, more important for the moment goal is to teach you how to do well on your BA/BO exam even though you have not done s—t all semester

We both understand that your exam is going to be different from the exam I give, and will be different from the exams taken by others relying on this book. What Professors Adams puts in his Corporations exams at Minnesota is different from what Professor Yuille puts in her Business Associations exam at Northeastern

This book is being written for students of all the various Professors Adams and Yuille and. . . so may cover some topics that

[1] My efforts to persuade my bosses at West Academic to entitle this book "A Short and Happy Guide to Business Associations FINAL EXAMS" were not successful. Guess that was not sufficiently "Academic."

your professor did not cover—topics you can skip. For example, if your professor assumed that you learned agency in your contracts and torts courses and so did not cover agency in BA/BO, skip Chapter 1. For the rest of you, here is what you need to know about agency. . .

PART 1

Fundamentals of All Business Organizations

CHAPTER 1

What You Need to Know About Agency

Large businesses like McDonald's Corporation have officers and other employees who act on behalf of McDonald's. The legal impact on McDonald's of what these officers and other employees do is governed by agency law.

Small businesses like Bubba's Barbecue, LLC, also have people who act on behalf of Bubba's. And, the legal impact on Bubba's Barbecue of what these people do is also governed by agency law.

There are five agency law questions that you need to be able to answer.

1. Where Does Agency Law Come from?

Agency law is basically common law. Law school B.A. courses emphasize the Restatements. Some professors use the Restatement (Second) of Agency; others teach the Restatement (Third). Fortunately, there are very few substantive differences between the two that are relevant to answering likely exam questions.

2. When Does an Agency Relationship Exist?

An agency relationship requires (i) one person acting on behalf of another—e.g., Ronald who is called the agent is acting on behalf of McDonald's which is called the princip**al** [NOTE THE "**AL**." YOU LOSE YOUR PROFESSOR'S TRUST AND CONFIDENCE IN YOUR ANSWERS IF YOU REFER TO AGENTS AND "PRINCIPL**ES**" ON YOUR EXAM]; (ii) the agent (A) is acting subject to the principal's (P) control (iii) and both A and P have consented to (i) and (ii).

3. What Is the Relevance of Agency Law to Liability on Contracts?

Here is the fact pattern to watch for: A contracts on behalf of P with T. More specifically, A contracts to buy goods or services for P from T.

The most commonly asked question arising from this fact pattern is whether the principal P is liable on a contract entered into by P's agent A and some third party, T. The critical word in answering this question is "authority."

P is liable for contracts made by A if P authorized A to make the contract for P. One more time—P authorized. To find the necessary authorization to hold principal P liable for a contract made by agent A, look for words of the principal P.

The two most common forms of authority are (1) actual authority and (2) apparent authority.

Actual authority arises from communications between P and A. Through P's words or conduct, P communicated to A that A could and should enter into contracts such as this contract with T.

Apparent authority arises from communications between P and T. Through P's words or conduct, P communicated to T that A could enter into such contracts as A's contract with T.

If you now understand actual and apparent authority, then you understand the following rules:

(1) an agent cannot create authority—P, not A, is the source of A's authority to contract for P;

(2) an agent can have both actual and apparent authority to enter into a contract;

(3) an agent's apparent authority can be different from and even broader than that agent's actual authority.

For example, P tells A that A has authority to buy grits on credit from T for P. P also tells T that A has authority to buy grits on credit from T for P. A thus has both actual and apparent authority.

Later, P tells A, but not T, that A is no longer authorized to buy grits on credit from T. A no longer has actual authority, but A still has apparent authority. If A buys more grits on credit from T, P will be liable on the contract to T.

It is important to understand actual and apparent authority. Actual and apparent authority are not only the basis for P's liability on contracts between A and T but are also the basis for P's rights on contracts between A and T. T will be liable to P if P would have been liable to T. Thus, if T fails to deliver the goods or services contracted for by A, P can enforce that contract against T so long as A was acting with actual or apparent authority.

Another question that commonly arises from the fact pattern involving agent A's contracting with third party T is whether the agent is liable to T on the contract. The key word in answering questions about the agent's liability is "disclosed."

If T had reason to know that A was acting as P's agent, then use the word "disclosed" and conclude that A is not liable on the contract he made with T. If, on the other hand, T did not know that A was acting as an agent, then use the word "undisclosed" and conclude that A is liable. And, if T knew that A was acting as an agent but did not know that A was acting as agent for P, use the words "partly disclosed" and conclude that A is liable on the contract.

Test yourself with the following question: Is it possible for both A and P to be liable on the contract A made with T? The answer is "of course"—if A was authorized and P was undisclosed, then both are liable on the contract with T.

4. What Is the Relevance of Agency Law to Liability for Torts?

You have done this before. In Torts. Do you remember "vicarious liability," "frolic or detour," and "master-servant?" If your class did the Restatement (Third), you can forget about "master-servant" and use the terms "employer" and "employee" instead.

And, you need to use these terms in the same unusual way as the Restatement (Third). A person can be an "employee" even though they do not receive wages from the "employer" if the "employer" has the "right to control" the employee's work.

Because liability for the negligence, recklessness, or wrongful acts of another is a part of Torts, it probably will not be a part of your Business Associations/Organizations final. At most, you might have:

(1) a multiple choice question or two requiring you to remember that an employer's liability for the torts of an employee depends on whether

  (i) the tortfeasor was acting within the scope of employment and

  (ii) whether the employer had the right to control

(2) a question on "apparent agency."

For purposes of tort law, apparent agency creates an agency relationship that does not actually exist. If, because of the words or conduct of P, T relies on A, believing that A is subject to P's control, then P is liable for A's torts.

Apparent agency has been used to hold a franchisor, such as McDonald's, liable for the torts of an employee of a franchisee because the advertising and other actions of McDonald's led the tort victim to believe that the restaurant was owned by McDonald's, not the franchisee, so that the tort victim believed that the tortfeasor was an "employee" of McDonald's.

Do not confuse "apparent agency" with "apparent authority." "Apparent authority" is a Contracts concept, expanding the authority of an actual agent. "Apparent agency" is a Torts concepts, expanding vicarious tort liability to the Torts of someone who is not actually an agent.

5. What Are the Duties That an Agent Owes to His Principal?

Agency is a fiduciary relationship between the agent and the principal. In general, an agent must act loyally and carefully. We will learn more about fiduciary duties and the duty of loyalty and care when we learn about partners who are agents of partnerships and officers who are agents of corporations (and directors of corporations who are not agents of corporations).

CHAPTER 2

What You Need to Know About Financial Statements

IF YOUR PROFESSOR SPENT CLASS TIME ON BALANCE SHEETS, INCOME STATEMENTS AND CASH FLOW STATEMENTS, then you need to know the answers to the following questions.

1. What Is a Balance Sheet?

A balance sheet compares (and balances) assets, i.e., what a business owns, and debts, i.e., what a business owes, to determine owner's equity, i.e., the book value of the business on a particular date. If, on April 5, 2026, Bubba's Burritos has assets of 1,000 and debts of 600, then Bubba's Burritos owner equity will be 400.

Think about the limited value of the information in the balance sheet. Is there any way that we can know that the assets would sell for 1,000? Is there any way that the value of Bubba's Burritos business is worth far more than the value of Bubba's Burritos assets? What if Bubba' Burritos assets are limited to food and a food truck—a food truck that is constantly surrounded by customers, waiting patiently to pay lots of bucks for Bubba's Burritos burritos?

2. What Is an Income Statement a/k/a Earnings Statement?

While the balance sheet speaks to a business's assets and liabilities at a particular date such as April 5, 2026, an income statement covers its business activities for a specific period of time—usually a year. The income statement tells you a business's profits or losses over that period by listing the business's earnings and business's expenses. If, during the calendar 2026, Bubba's Burritos generated revenue of 100 and paid out expenses of 80, its income was 20.

Watch for the fact pattern in which Bubba's Burritos spent 30 in 2026for equipment that it will be able to use for 6 years. Then 5 (30/6) can be considered the 2026 expense.

3. What Is a Cash Flow Statement?

A cash flow statement is like an income statement, only slightly different. Like an income statement, a cash flow statement looks at a business's financial performance over a specific time period—usually a year.

As the title suggests, the focus is on cash. Not all earnings but instead only cash earned. Not all expenses but only cash expended.

To review, a 100 credit sale on December 30, 2026, would be included in the 2021 income statement but not in the 2026 cash flow statement. A payment of 30 for equipment with a 6-year useful life would be reflected as 30 less cash in the cash flow statement.

CHAPTER 3

What You Need to Know About Your Course Title

Your course is not called "Business." It is called "Business Associations" or "Business Organizations" or "Corporations."

You are not going to be tested about the legal problems of a business. Rather the questions are limited to the legal problems of a business unique to doing business as a "business association" or "business organization." Thus, the course name.

1. What Is a Sole Proprietorship?

Most businesses are sole proprietorships. A business that is a sole proprietorship is not a business association or organization. Your course and your exam are not about sole proprietorships. There is not a body of "sole proprietorship law."

At most, you need to know when a business is a sole proprietorship. Look for two facts. A business is a sole proprietorship if

(1) the business has only one owner (a sole proprietorship can have multiple employees but only one owner);

(2) the business has not filed the necessary papers with the appropriate state government agency to be a corporation or a limited liability company.

2. What Are the Forms of Business Associations/Organizations?

As you will learn corporations and limited liability companies are business associations/business organizations. And, while corporations and limited liability companies usually have multiple owners, corporations and limited liability companies can exist with only one owner.

Unlike sole proprietorships, corporations, and limited liability companies, partnerships and limited partnerships must have more than one owner. Partnerships are also business associations/organizations. So are limited partnerships.

3. What Are the Sources of the Laws Governing Business Associations/Organizations?

Each state has statutes governing the operation of a business that is a partnership, a corporation, a limited partnership or a limited liability company. Each such state statute treats the business as a legal entity, separate from and additional to its owners for at least some purposes. So, for example, if Bubba's Burritos, Inc., has three owners (Larry, Moe, and Curly), then, for most purposes, there are four legal entities (Larry, Moe, Curly, and Bubba's Burritos).

And each partnership, each corporation, and each limited liability company has one or more agreements governing its operations. These agreements include partnership agreements, articles of incorporation, and operating agreements.

Some statutory provisions are merely default rules—applicable only if the partnership agreement, articles of incorporation or operating agreement does not otherwise provide. Other statutory provisions create duties that cannot be contracted away. These are probably going to be covered on your exam and so are certain to be covered in the next parts of this book.

PART 2

Partnerships

CHAPTER 4

What You Need to Know About the Legal Attributes of a Partnership

The legal attributes of a partnership can be found primarily in the statutes of the state where the partnership is located. Most state statutes are modeled after either the Uniform Partnership Act (UPA) or the Revised Uniform Partnership Act (RUPA). There have been a number of revisions of RUPA. Most BA/BO classes use statutory supplements that contain RUPA(1997) (Last Amendment 2013) so that is what I will use in this book.

UPA is commonly labeled as an "aggregate-based statute." RUPA is commonly referred to as an "entity-based statute."

You need to know the terms "entity" and "aggregate" even if your class only covered UPA or only covered RUPA.

1. Why Is a Partnership Generally Considered an "Entity"?

A partnership is an "entity" to the extent that relevant state law treats it as a separate person.

People can sue or be sued in their own name. Under both UPA and RUPA, a partnership can sue or be sued in its own name.

People can own property. Under UPA and RUPA, a partnership can own property. If Larry, Moe, and Curly are the partners in Bubba's Burritos Partnership (BBP), BBP can own property such as Redacre. And, if BBP owns Redacre, then Larry, Moe, or Curly cannot take or sell Redacre. A partner can only use partnership property for partnership purposes, not for personal gain.

People can incur debt. And, if people do not pay their debts, their creditors can use the judicial process to collect the debts from the debtor's property. Under UPA or RUPA, BBP can incur debt. And, if BBP does not pay its debts, BBP's creditors can use the judicial process to collect judgments from BBP's property, such as Redacre.

2. Why Is a Partnership Sometimes Considered an "Aggregate" and Not an "Entity"?

A partnership is an "aggregate" to the extent that the law treats it as merely an aggregate of its owners rather than as a separate person. The most important example of a federal law treating a partnership as an aggregate is the Internal Revenue Code. For example, a partnership such as BBP does not pay taxes. The income from BBP is "passed through" to its partners, Larry, Moe, and Curly.

The most important example of state law treating a partnership as an aggregate is the statutory rule that partners are personally liable for the partnership's debts. Under both UPA and

RUPA, BBP's creditors can collect what the BBP partnership owes them from BBP's partners, if BBP's creditors are unable to satisfy their judgments in full from BBP's property.

The most important aggregate/entity distinction between UPA and RUPA is the effect of a partner's leaving the partnership. More about that later.

CHAPTER 5

What You Need to Know About Starting a Partnership

1. How Do You Determine Whether a Business Is Structured as a Partnership?

If two or more people are co-owners of a for profit business that is not a corporation or a limited liability company, that business is a partnership. Please read that sentence again. Four big "take-aways."

First, a partnership requires two or more co-owners. No such thing as a one-person partnership.

The co-owners of a partnership do not have to be flesh and blood people. A legal entity such as a corporation or a limited liability company can be a partner. For example, Acme, Inc. and Baker Corp. could form a partnership and be the only partners in that partnership.

Second, a partnership is the default form of association/organization for a business with two or more owners. If a business with two or more owners has not met the requirements for being a corporation or a limited liability company, then it is a partnership.

Third, the most important requirement for the formation of a partnership is co-ownership.

And, the most important fact in determining whether people are co-owners is sharing profits. If Larry, Moe, and Curly are sharing BBP's profits, that creates a rebuttable presumption that they are partners.

That rebuttable presumption can of course be rebutted. For example, a creditor can share in a business's profits without being deemed a co-owner and thus a partner.

Co-ownership also involves control over the business's affairs. *Martin v. Peyton,* included in many casebooks, concluded that a lender who was sharing in the profits was not a partner because it "may not initiate any transactions as a partner may do."

Fourth, no formal act is required to start a partnership. Nothing needs to be filed by the owners; nothing needs to be recorded or done by the state.

While no formal acts are required to create a partnership, two formal acts are likely to appear in your exam fact patterns: (1) partnership agreements and (2) partners' accounts.

2. What Is the Importance of a Partnership Agreement?

A partnership agreement is an agreement among the partners and between the partnership and the partners.

If Gertrude Stein were to read that last sentence, she might accuse me of plagiarism. Just as a "rose is a rose," a "partnership agreement is an agreement among the partners. . . ."

There are two important things for you to know about partnership agreements:

First, a partnership agreement does not have to be in writing or be based on words. A partnership agreement can be based, in whole or in part, on conduct, RUPA 101(7).

Second, and more important, the partnership agreement can change much of the statutory partnership law that would otherwise govern disputes among the partners and between the partnership and the partners, RUPA 103(a).

If the exam question is about the relative rights and duties of partner Larry and partnership BBP, or the rights and duties of partners Larry and Moe to each other, then look first for information about what the partners have agreed to and second look to RUPA 103. On the other hand, if the exam question is a dispute between the partnership or one of more partners and some third party who is not a partner, then the provisions in the partnership agreement are irrelevant and you look to RUPA.

3. What Are Partners' Accounts?

Partners' accounts are relevant if the exam question involves dissolution, i.e., end, of a partnership. Partners' accounts show the money and other property that a partner has invested in the partnership, and the money or other distributions that a partner has received from the partnership. If Moe invests 100 in BBP and later receives 40 as his share of BBP's profits, then Moe's partner's account would show a positive balance of 60.

Under some partnership statutes, a partner's account is credited to show property that partner contributed to the partnership, as well as cash that partner invested in the partnership, but not the value of services that partner contributed. The following hypothetical illustrates the application of such a statute. Moe invests 1000 in BBP; Larry deeds Redacre worth 400 to BBP; and Curly works for BBP without pay. Moe's partnership account would be credited with 1000; Larry's partnership account would be credited at 400; and Curly's partnership account would still be at 0 as no partnership account credit would be given for services contributed by Curly to the partnership.

This seems unfair. Many casebooks include the case of *Kovacik v. Reed*, in which Reed invested $10,000 in a home remodeling partnership and Kovacik contributed his labor. The California Supreme Court concluded that the partners, by their agreement to share profits and losses equally, had in essence agreed that the labor contributed by Kovacik was to be valued the same in the partnership accounts as the capital invested by Reed.[1]

The dispute in *Kovacik v. Reed* arose at the dissolution of the partnership. When we study partnership dissolution in Chapter 10, we will see that the amounts in BBP's various partners' accounts is important when BBP dissolves and makes final distributions to its partners.

---

[1] Recall that most of the UPA and RUPA rules governing the relative rights of partners and the partnership are "default rules"—rules that can be changed by agreement of the parties. Accordingly, this "implied" (court-supplied?) agreement between Kovacik and Reed could change any statutory rule that regarding services and partnership accounts.

CHAPTER 6

What You Need to Know About Operating a Business as a Partnership

There are four different but related questions that can be asked about operating a business as a partnership. You need to know how to respond to questions about (i) who can incur debts for a partnership, (ii) who is liable for partnership debts, (iii) who makes decisions for the partnership and (iv) what are the duties of such decision-makers.

1. First: Who Can Incur Debts for a Partnership?

By statute, each partner is an agent of the partnership. RUPA 301 provides in pertinent part:

> 1. Each partner is an agent of the partnership for the purpose of its business. An act of a partner, including the execution of an instrument in the partnership name, for apparently carrying on in the ordinary course the partnership business or business of the

kind carried on by the partnership binds the partnership, unless the partner had no authority to act for the partnership in the particular matter and the person with whom the partner was dealing knew or had received a notification that the partner lacked authority.

2. An act of a partner which is not apparently for carrying on in the ordinary course the partnership business or business of the kind carried on by the partnership binds the partnership only if the act was authorized by the other partners.

Section 9 of UPA is virtually identical.

Some professors refer to the authority resulting from these statutes as "actual authority." Others describe the authority as "apparent authority." Use whichever label your professor prefers.

More important, know that

(1) General rule: any partner has authority to enter into contract that is "ordinary course" for that partnership's business.

(2) Exception: a partner does not have authority to enter into a contract that is in the "ordinary course" for that partnership's business if the partnership agreement provides that the partner does not have authority to enter into that contract and the other party to the contract knows or has reason to know of this limitation.

Thus if the only facts in the exam fact pattern are that (i) Don and Phil are the two partners in the Everly Brothers Barbecue Partnership (EBP), (ii) the EBP is in the business of barbecuing brisket and (iii) partner Don buys brisket on credit for the EBP from C, that debt to C for brisket is a debt of the partnership. And, as you will see in the next part, C can collect that partnership debt from EBP or from Don and Phil.

2. Second: Who Is Liable for a Partnership's Debts to Third Parties?

A partnership can be held liable for its debts arising from the contracts made by its partners or torts committed by its partners. If, for example V, a client of the Three Stooges law partnership (TSLP), proves that lawyer partner Moe committed malpractice and obtains a $150,000 judgment, then V can recover from the BBP partnership.

And, all of the partners are liable for the debts of a partnership. Under the facts in the prior paragraph, V can also recover from the three partners in TSLP. All the partners. Not just the tortfeasor partner. V could recover from partner Shemp for partner Moe.

It will be less complicated procedurally for V to collect the partnership tort debt from the partnership TSLP than from non-tortfeasor/partner Shemp. Under RUPA, in order for a creditor of the TSLP partnership such as V to collect from a partner such as Shemp, V must have not only a judgment against both the partnership, TSLP, and a judgment against the partner, Shemp but also have exhausted efforts to collect from TSLP before being able to collect TSLP's debt from partner Shemp.

And, if V collects TSLP's $150,000 debt from Shemp then Shemp would have a right of indemnity against TSLP and a right of contribution from the other partners Moe and Curly. To do the math, if TSLP is not able to repay Shemp any of the $150,000, then Shemp could compel Moe and Curly to contribute $50,000 each to Shemp. Partnership agreements cannot eliminate or limit partners' possible liability for the debts of a partnership. A partnership agreement cannot "restrict the rights of a person other than a partner," RUPA 105(c)(17).

3. Third: Who Makes Decisions for the Partnership?

In the real world, the answer to the question of who makes decisions for the partnership is found in the partnership agreement. In the unreal world of a law school exam, you will find the answer in the partnership statute's default rules. And here are the five exam-important statutory default rules. Unless the partnership agreement otherwise provides

(1) Regardless of how much or little various partners may have contributed to the partnership, each partner has one vote;

(2) Ordinary course matters may be decided by a majority of the partners;

(3) Non-ordinary course matters require consent of all partners;

(4) Admission of a new partner requires consent of all partners; and

(5) Amendment of the partnership agreement requires consent of all partners.

Again, these five rules are default rules—legally relevant only if not contradicted by the partnership agreement. A partnership agreement can provide for a very different decision-making structure. For example, partnership agreements can provide for a managing partner who makes all decisions.

4. Fourth: What Are the Legal Duties of a Partnership's Decision-Makers?

A partner is an agent of the partnership. And, we know from agency law that an agent owes her principal fiduciary duties.

And we know from partnership statutes and case law that a partner owes the partnership and other partners a fiduciary duty. The language of RUPA 409 is especially instructive (especially if your "instructor" assigned the section):

a. The only fiduciary duties a partner owes to the partnership and the other partners are the duty of loyalty and the duty of care set forth in 409 subsections b and c.

b. A partner's duty of loyalty to the partnership and the other partners includes the duties:

    1. To account to the partnership . . . for . . .any property, profit, or benefit derived by the partner . . . from the appropriation of a partnership opportunity;

    2. To refrain from dealing with the partnership in the conduct . . . of the partnership business as or on behalf of a party having an interest adverse to the partnership; and

    3. To refrain from competing with the partnership in the conduct of the partnership business before the dissolution of the partnership.

c. A partner's duty of care to the partnership and the other partners in the conduct and winding up of the partnership business is limited to refraining from engaging in grossly negligent or reckless conduct, intentional misconduct, or a knowing violation of law.

d. A partner shall discharge the duties to the partnership and the other partners under this act or under the partnership agreement and exercise any rights consistent with the contractual obligation of good faith and fair dealing.

4.1. What Do You Need to Know About a Partner's Duty of Care?

Not much.

RUPA 404(a) first states that fiduciary duty includes a duty of care. The duty of care is a very limited duty—limited by RUPA 404(c) to gross negligence or worse. A partner does not breach her duty of care to the partnership and her partners for mere negligence.

You will need to know more about a director's duty of care. That's Chapter 17. And a lot of the legal concepts limiting litigation alleging breach of director's duty of care—such as business judgment rule—also limit litigation alleging breach of a partner's duty of care.

4.2. What Do You Need to Know About a Partner's Duty of Loyalty?

If essay questions on your exam raise issues of partner's fiduciary duties, they will likely be duty of loyalty issues. In general, look for a fact pattern in which a partner benefitted financially at a cost to the partnership.

More specifically, watch for the following three possible fact patterns: (1) a partner's taking for herself a business opportunity that belongs to the partnership (which is covered by RUPA 409(b)(1)), or (2) a partner improperly profiting from a deal she or some related party made with the partnership (which is covered by RUPA 409(b)(2)), or (3) a partner's competing with the partnership while still a partner (which is covered by RUPA 409(b)(3)).

Meinhard v. Salmon, involved fact pattern (1). Numerous law professors consider *Meinhard v. Salmon* to be the most important business associations/organizations case ever. If your professor is in that number, read the next few paragraphs carefully.

Meinhard and Salmon formed what the court called a joint venture (and what today law professors would call a partnership[1]) to lease and improve a building owned by Gerry. Meinhard was the "behind the scenes money-man." Salmon was the manager or what the court repeatedly called the "managing coadventurer."

Shortly before the end of the lease, Gerry approached Salmon about investing in, leasing, and managing a new, larger project involving a replacement building and adjacent land. Salmon took this opportunity for himself. Meinhard sued Salmon for being cut out of the deal.

Writing for a divided Court of Appeals of New York, Cardozo found that Salmon breached his duty of loyalty. The opinion is rich with colorful, frequently quoted phrases.

More exam-important are the following limiting facts near the end of Cardozo's opinion: (1) the "relation between the business conducted by the manager and the opportunity brought to him as an incident of management" and (2) the "subject matter of the new lease was an extension and an enlargement of the subject-matter of the old one."

And, so, if on your exam fact pattern, the partner Salmon gets the opportunity because his daughter is on the same soccer team as Gerry's kid, there is no breach of fiduciary duty by taking a

[1] Remember if a business has two or more owners and is not a corporation or a limited liability company then it is a partnership.

partnership opportunity. The opportunity was not "brought to him as an incident of management."

Or, if on your exam fact pattern. the subject matter of the new opportunity for partner Salmon—opening a Glatt Kosher Chinese restaurant—is significantly different from the subject matter of the old one—improving and operating a building—no breach. The Chinese restaurant was not an "extension and enlargement of the subject-matter (building management) of the old one."

4.3. *Why Is "Good Faith and Fair Dealing" Much Less Important?*

Look to section 409(d) and the phrase "contractual obligation of good faith and fair dealing." It is not clear what, if anything, that language adds to the duty of loyalty and the duty of care. And the language of the last sentence is about all that you can add concerning "good faith and fair dealing" in answering an exam question about a partner's duty to the partnership and other partners.

4.4. *What Is the Importance of Language in the Partnership Agreement in Determining a Partner's Legal Duties?*

In answering an exam question about a partner's duties to the partnership and other partners, it is necessary to look not only to RUPA or UPA and case law, but also to information in the exam question about the language in the partnership agreement. While a partnership agreement cannot eliminate a partner's duty of care or duty loyalty, a partnership agreement may limit these duties if the limitations are not "manifestly unreasonable." RUPA 105(d)(3).

This would seem to mean that the partnership agreement could permit a partner's competing with the partnership or taking partnership opportunities for herself, so long as not "manifestly unreasonable. Your guess is as good as mine as to what "manifestly unreasonable" means."[2]

[2] Unless your professor is "manifestly unreasonable," your grade on a law school exam question will not depend on your divining what a court would or would not find to be "manifestly unreasonable." You just need to know that a partnership agreement's limitations on a partner's duty of loyalty are subject to a "not manifestly unreasonable" limitation and that "manifestly unreasonable" is worse than merely unreasonable. My wife and sons and coauthors and friends and . . . regularly tell me that I am being "unreasonable." They save "manifestly unreasonable" for the times that I . . .

CHAPTER 7

What You Need to Know About a Partnership's Adding New Partners

Growth of a business often requires additional funding. One common source of such funding is new investors.

While doing law school exam questions about partnerships' seeking new investors it is important to:

(1) regard the investor in a partnership business as a partner; and

(2) determine whether the question is

 (i) whether the person can become a partner; or

 (ii) what are the legal obligations of a person who becomes a new partner; or

 (iii) both (i) and (ii); and

(3) look for what the fact pattern tells you about partnership agreement provisions relating to new partners; and

(4) finding no such provisions apply the partnership law default rules for new partners.

1. Who Determines Whether a New Partner Can Be Added?

The partnership statutes' default rules, which are applicable where the partnership agreement does not otherwise provide, state that a person can become a new partner of an existing partnership only if all of the existing partners consent. The reasons for the rule are (1) each partner is an agent for the partnership, (2) each partner can thereby create contract or tort liability for the partnership and (3) each partner is personally liable for the debts of the partnership. In sum, each partner has personal liability exposure for the partnership-related activities of all other partners.

Thus, if in 2026, Shemp wants to invest 100 in BBP and become the fourth BBP partner, the three existing partners would have to approve. And, once Shemp became a partner, Shemp's partnership related activities can result in partnership debts and personal liability exposure to the other partners for such debts.

2. What Are the Debt Obligations of a New Partner?

And, if, in 2026, Shemp became a partner in already existing BBP, Shemp would not be liable for debts incurred prior to the date in 2026 that Shemp became a partner, absent an agreement to the contrary. A new partner is not personally liable on debts incurred by the partnership before they became a partner.

To review, think about the impact on BBP's balance sheet of Shemp's investing 100 in BBP and becoming a new partner. On the left hand side of the balance sheet, assets would be increased by 100. On the right hand side of the balance sheet, equity would be increased by 100. Shemp's becoming a partner by investing 100 would in essence increase the size of the "asset pie" available to the partners but would also increase the number of partners who partake in that pie.

Shemp's becoming a partner by investing 100 would not increase the amount of the partnership's debt, and Shemp would not be liable for the debts that the partnership had incurred before Shemp became a partner. Shemp would, of course, be liable just as any other partner, for the later debts of the partnership.

CHAPTER 8

What You Need to Know About Partners' Making Money

Partners can make money by (1) working for the partnership for a salary and (2) sharing in partnership profits; or (3) selling their partnership interest at a profit.

1. When Is a Partner Entitled to a Salary?

A partner who is employed by the partnership has a right to salary payments from the partnership pursuant to that employment agreement. Don't be misled by RUPA 401(j)—"a partner is not entitled to remuneration for services performed for the partnership." Again, just a default rule. Partners can and do regularly agree, by words or conduct, that the partnership will pay salaries to all or merely some of the partners.

2. How and When Do Partners Share in the Partnership's Profits?

Similarly, RUPA 401(a)—"partner is entitled to an equal share of the partnership distributions"—is just a default rule, displaced by relevant partnership agreement provisions. And partnership agreements almost always provide (i) who decides when a partnership's profits are to be distributed and (2) how such a distribution is to be allocated among the partners. If Larry has invested 100 in BBP and works for BBP 50 hours a week, and Moe has invested 60 in BBP and works for BBP 30 hours a week and Curly has invested 10 in BBP and works for BBP 10 hours a week, an equal distribution of profits under the UPA or RUPA default rule would be a real poke in the eye for Larry.

3. What Can a Partner Sell Their Interest to Third Parties?

Things get more complicated when a partner tries to make money by selling their interest in the partnership. First, there are the obvious business problems of finding a buyer. Second, and more exam-important, is the legal rule that, unless all other partners agree, a partner can only sell or otherwise transfer their own "transferable interest."

For this last rule to make sense, you need to recall a few concepts and then learn this new concept of "transferable interest." Recall that (i) each partner has decision-making power, (ii) each partner has a right to share in partnership distributions, (iii) each partner is an agent of the partnership and can obligate the partnership on contracts, (iv) a partner's wrongdoing while conducting partnership business can create partnership obligations, and (v) each partner has personal liability for these partnership contract and tort obligations. And, recall that because of (iii), (iv) and (v) a partnership can add a new partner only if all existing partners agree.

Similarly, because of (iii), (iv) and (v) above, a partner can sell only their financial rights unless a partnership agreement otherwise provides or all partners otherwise agree. Under RUPA default rules, a partner's financial interest is their "transferable interest"—that and nothing more.

Thus, if Curly, a BBP partner, sells his partnership interest to Shemp, all that Shemp gets is the right to receive the BBP distributions that Curly would otherwise be entitled to. Shemp is not a partner. Curly retains the rights of a partner other than the right to distributions and the duties of a partner, including personal liability for partnership debts, RUPA 503(f).

So, if after Curly sells his transferable interest in BBP to Shemp, BBP decides to lease a building, Curly and not Shemp would be part of that decision-making process. And Curly, not Shemp, would have personal liability on the lease if BBP defaults.

Because of the business and legal problems of a partner's making money by selling their partnership interest to a third party, RUPA provides for dissociation. Dissociation is important.

CHAPTER 9

What You Need to Know About Dissociation

You don't need to know anything about "dissociation" if your professor only covered UPA. The addition of "dissociation" is one of the most important differences between UPA and RUPA.

If the partnership part of your course did cover RUPA and dissociation, then you need to know four things about dissociation: (i) what dissociation is, (ii) the legal consequences of dissociation, (iii) the differences between the power to dissociate and the right to dissociate, and (iv) the relationship and possible lack of relationship between dissociation and dissolution.

1. What Is Dissociation?

Dissociation is the term RUPA uses for a partner's withdrawing from the partnership. It's the end game for a partner. If Moe dissociates from TSLP on January 15, 2026, then, as of January 15, 2026, Moe is no longer a TSLP partner.

Dissociation can be voluntary or involuntary. The most common examples of involuntary dissociation are bankruptcy of a partner, death of a partner who is an individual, and expulsion.

2. What Are the Legal Consequences of Dissociation?

As noted above, when Moe dissociated on January 15th, he ceased being a partner. Remember a partner is liable for the debts of the partnership. Moe was a partner until January 15th Moe would have the same liability as any remaining BBP partner for debts BBP incurred before Moe's April 5 dissociation.

Also, remember a partner owes a duty of loyalty to the partnership which means, inter alia, that a partner cannot compete with the partnership. After January, Moe can compete with TSLP.

And, remember, a partner participates in partnership decision-making. Moe's rights to participate in the management and conduct of TSLP's business end with Moe's January 15th dissociation.

Remember also that a partner is an agent for the partnership. While Moe's January 15th dissociation terminates any actual authority arising from his status as partner, he still can have apparent authority.

Assume that (i) Moe was the TSLP partner who bought law books for the partnership on credit from West Academic and (ii) Moe dissociates from TSLP on January 15th and (iii) Moe contracts to buy lawbooks on credit for TSLP from West Academic on February 16th. TSLP would be contractually obligated to West Academic on the February 16th contract if West Academic reasonably believed that Moe was still a partner.

The final and most "exam-important" legal consequence of dissociation is that the dissociating partner is entitled to a buyout of their partnership interest by the partnership. Partnership agreements typically provide the method of determining the amount to be paid to a dissociating partner. If, as is likely in exam fact patterns, there is no such partnership provision, RUPA 701(b) provides that the dissociating partner is to be paid the greater of their share of either (i) the liquidation value of the partnership or (ii) the going concern value of the partnership.

3. What Are the Differences Between the Power to Dissociate and the Right to Dissociate?

Under RUPA, a partner can always dissociate. Moe can dissociate from TSLP on January 15, 2026, even if the partnership agreement provides that no partner can dissociate until 2028. A partner always has the power to dissociate.

While a partner always has the power to dissociate, they do not always have the right to dissociate. A dissociation is wrongful if, as in the prior paragraph, it breaches an express provision in the partnership agreement.

Moreover, a partner's dissociation is wrongful if the partnership agreement provides that that the partnership is to exist for a specific term or until the completion of a particular undertaking. If, for example, the LockeGate partnership agreement provides that the LockeGate partnership is to continue until all of the lots in the LockeGate gated community have been sold, a LockeGate partner would have the power to dissociate before then, but that dissociation would be wrong.

Most partnerships are "at-will" partnerships. In other words, most partnership agreements do not provide that the existence of the partnership is limited to a particular term of time or ends only on the completion of a particular undertaking. Accordingly, most partner dissociations are not wrongful.

If a partner's dissociation is wrongful, then any damages to the partnership caused by the wrongful dissociation reduces the buyout amount that partner receives from the partnership. More importantly, if a partner wrongfully dissociates before the expiration of the partnership's stated term or completion of the partnership's stated undertaking, she does not necessarily receive her buyout payment from the partnership immediately. If a partner's dissociation is wrongful, then the partnership can postpone the buyout payment until the conclusion of the term or undertaking, unless the dissociating partner can prove that earlier payment will not result in hardship to the partnership.

4. What Is the Relationship and Possible Lack of Relationship Between Dissociation and Dissolution?

Dissociation is in essence the "end game" for a partner. When Moe dissociates, withdrawing as a partner from TSLP, he is ending his career as a partner of TSLP.

Dissolution is in essence the "end game" for the partnership. Or at least the beginning of the end for partnership. When BBP dissolves, it is taking the first step to ending its life as a partnership business.

Recall that under UPA, there is no dissociation. And, recall that under UPA a partnership was generally viewed as merely an aggregate of its partners—not a separate entity. Under UPA, the LSP partnership is no more than a combination of its partners, Shemp, Moe, and Curly.

Accordingly under UPA, withdrawal—the end of game for one partner—results in dissolution—the end game for the partnership. Since UPA viewed TSLP as no more than a combination of Shemp, Moe, and Curly, TSLP could not continue to exist after Moe's withdrawal. Without Moe, the aggregate of Shemp, Moe, and Curly no longer exists. Again, the UPA rule is that a partner's withdrawal triggers dissolution.

RUPA, on the other hand, views TSLP as an entity, separate from Shemp, Moe, and Curly. Thus, TSLP can exist even after Moe withdraws from TSLP by exercising his RUPA power to dissociate.

The RUPA rule that a partner's withdrawal from a partnership does not trigger dissolution is subject to two exceptions that might be important on your exam. First, in a RUPA at-will partnership, a partner who chooses to dissociate can compel dissolution. Second, in a RUPA partnership for a term or particular undertaking, a partner's death or wrongful dissociation gives half or more of the remaining partners the power to cause dissolution of the partnership.

CHAPTER 10

What Do You Need to Know About Partnership Dissolution?

You need to know five things about dissolution: (i) what other than a partner's withdrawal can effect a dissolution of a partnership, (ii) what are the effects of partnership dissolution on the operation of the partnership, (iii) what are the effects of partnership dissolution on the partnership's creditors, (iv) what are the effects of partnership dissolution on the partners, and (v) what is the possible relationship between partnership dissolution and a partner's breach of their fiduciary duty.

1. What Other than a Partner's Withdrawal Can Affect a Dissolution of the Partnership?

RUPA 801 lists the "events causing dissolution." For example, all the partners can agree on dissolution. And, if the partnership agreement so provides, less than all of the partners can agree on dissolution. Your prof might have called this a "voluntary dissolution."

And one or more partners can ask a court to order the dissolution of the partnership. Your prof might have called this "involuntary dissolution" or "judicial; dissolution.

UPA and RUPA set out grounds for judicial dissolution. The statutory grounds for judicial dissolution of a partnership are premised on highly subjective facts—e.g., "economic purpose of the partnership likely to be unreasonably frustrated" or "not reasonably practicable to carry on the partnership business." Accordingly, an exam question on judicial dissolution is likely to be an essay question that requires you to compare the facts in the question with the facts in the assigned cases on judicial dissolution.

2. What Are the Effects of Partnership Dissolution on the Operation of the Partnership?

Dissolution is not exactly the "end game" for a partnership's business operations. Again, dissolution is more the beginning of the end of the business operations of the partnership than the actual end.

After dissolution, the next step under RUPA 802 is winding up the business of the partnership. In essence, winding up means that the partnership can finish up old business, but the dissolving partnership cannot take in new business. After dissolution, under RUPA 804, partners retain actual authority only to enter into transactions designed to terminate the business but may have broader apparent authority.

And, winding up typically involves the sale of partnership assets with the sale proceeds distributed first to creditors and then to partners and others holding transferable interests.

3. What Are the Effects of Partnership Dissolution on Creditors of the Partnership?

Remember what a balance sheet looks like? Assets on the left, debt above equity on the right? In other words, on a balance sheet, debt comes before equity.

Similarly, on dissolution of a partnership, the partnership's creditors must be paid in full before the partners recover any part of their investment.

A person can be both a partner and a creditor. For example, Moe might pay TSLP $10,000 to acquire a 1/3 partnership interest and later lend TSLP $3,000. Moe would thus be both a creditor and partner.

RUPA treats debts owed to partners no different from other debts. UPA requires a dissolving partnership to pay its other creditors first.

To illustrate, assume that TSLP owes $30,000, including the $3,000 owed to Moe. If the liquidation of TSLP's assets nets only $15,000, then Moe would receive $1,500 (3000 × 15,000/30,000) under RUPA and nothing under UPA.

Not only can a partner be a creditor of the partnership, but a partner can also (and more likely) be an additional debtor for the partnership's creditors. If the proceeds from the liquidation of the partnership's assets are not sufficient, then the partners are jointly and severally liable for any insufficiency.

4. What Are the Effects of Partnership Dissolution on the Partners?

We have just seen two of the three exam-important effects of partnership dissolution on the partners—first, limitation on partners' actual authority and, second, possible personal liability of partners to the partnership's creditors. The third effect of partnership dissolution on the partners—settlement of partnership accounts—is a little more complicated.

Recall that each partner has a partnership account that shows how much that partner invested in the partnership and how much that partner received from the partnership. In winding up a dissolving partnership, the partnership accounts must be settled after the partnership's creditors have been paid.

The easiest way to explain settlement of partnership accounts is through illustrations. For example, assume the following facts:

(1) Moe, Shemp, and Curly are the three partners in TSLP, a dissolving partnership.

(2) After the sale of TSLP assets and payment of all TSLP debts, there is a surplus (i.e. profits) of $15,000.

(3) The partnership agreement provides that profits and losses are to be shared equally.

(4) Moe's partnership account is at $65,000, Shemp's partnership account is at $30,000 and Curly's partnership account is at $-5000. (Curly invested $100,000 in TSLP and, while a TSLP partner, Curly received $105,000 from TSLP.)

If only the $15,000 of partnership funds are divided equally among the three, then the losses would not have been shared equally.

Do the math. Moe's partnership account shows that he has put $65,000 more into TSLP than he has taken out—his TSLP loss is $65,000. If Moe gets $5000 of the profits, Moe's loss is still $60,00. If Shemp, whose partnership account is at $30.000, gets $5,000 of the profits, his TSLP loss would be $25,000. Curly, on the other hand, would get gain $10,000 from TSLP if he gets $5,000 of the

TSLP profits since he had already received $5,000 more from TSLP than he had put in.

Now for the law part of settlement of partnership accounts. Remember the legal rule that partners are personally liable for the partnership's obligations to its creditors. Now for the "pocket part" to that legal rule: partners are also personally liable for the partnership's obligations to its partners.

TSLP's $15,000 left after paying its creditors is not enough to cover TSLP's $65,000 obligation to Moe on his partnership account, and TSLP's $30,000 obligation to Shemp on his partnership account. TSLP's partners must make up the difference.

And, so, again to do the math, TSLP's partnership account deficiencies total $90,000 ($65,000 + $30,000 - $5,000). And the partnership surplus is only $15,000, and so each partner should sustain a $25,000 loss ([90,000 - 15,000] / 3). If the $15,000 partnership surplus goes to Moe, then his loss will be $50,000. If Curly then pays Moe $25,000 and pays Shemp $5,000, then each of the three TSLP partners will have sustained a loss of $25,000 from being a TSLP partner.

5. What Is the Possible Relationship Between Partnership Dissolution and a Partner's Breach of Her Fiduciary Duty?

After a partnership completes the three stages of the dissolution process—(1) "dissolution," (2) "winding up" and (3) "termination"—the people who were partners no longer owe a fiduciary duty to the partnership or to the other partners. During the dissolution process, however, there are the same "old" fiduciary duties and new opportunities to breach those duties.

Watch especially for a fact pattern involving (i) a partnership at-will with strong, future business opportunities and (ii) dissolution of that partnership by the one partner with the ability to take advantage of those opportunities on her own. In *Page v. Page*, a case with such facts that it is included in several casebooks, the California Supreme Court stated: "A partner at will is not bound to remain in a partnership, . . . A partner may not however, . . . 'freeze out' a co-partner and appropriate the business to his own use. A partner may not dissolve a partnership to gain the benefits of the partnership for himself, unless he fully compensates his co-partner for his share of the prospective business opportunity."

Watch for that wonderfully descriptive phrase "freeze out." We will be using that and a lot of the stuff we learned about partnerships in the next part of the book on corporations.

PART 3

Corporations

Vocabulary is a big part of corporations law and a big part of your BA/BO test. You are going to lose points on multiple choice questions if you don't know all the terms your professor uses in the multiple choice answers; you are going to lose your professor's confidence if you misuse words in your answers to essay questions.

Here is a check list of words that will be used in Part 3 that you will need to use on your exam:

(1) People

a. promoter

b. incorporator

c. shareholder/stockholder

d. directors

e. officers

(2) Paper

a. subscription agreement

b. articles of incorporation/certificate of incorporation

c. bylaws

d. proxy

e. voting trust

f. voting agreement

g. shareholders agreement

h. registration statement (Form S-1)

(3) Special types of corporations

a. foreign

b. close

c. public

d. de jure

e. de facto

f. corporation by estoppel

g. parent

h. subsidiary

i. brother/sister

j. 34 Act Company

(4) Stock terms

a. authorized

b. issued

c. outstanding

d. class of stock

e. preferred/common

f. par/no par

g. watered

h. preemptive rights

i. cumulative voting

j. record owner

k. record date

l. dissenting shareholder's right of appraisal

(5) Dividends

a. preferred

b. participating

c. cumulative

d. stated capital

(6) Case law concepts

a. internal affairs doctrine

b. piercing the corporate veil

c. enterprise liability

d. business judgment rule

e. de facto merger

(7) Litigation concepts

a. duty of care

b. duty of loyalty

c. usurping a corporate opportunity

d. interested director transaction

e. shareholder derivative suit

f. direct suits

g. demand

h. special Litigation Committee

CHAPTER 11

What You Need to Know About the Legal Attributes of a Corporation

There once was an unsuccessful presidential candidate who said that a corporation is a person. And a bunch of Supreme Court Justices who said the same thing. Sort of.[1]

1. Why Is It Important That a Corporation Is a Legal "Person"?

More important for your BA/BO exam are the statutes and cases that say that a corporation is a legal entity, legally separate and distinct from the person(s) who own it and the persons who run it. This means:

- Corporations own property;
- Corporations pay taxes;

[1] For example, a majority of the Justices concluded that corporations—or at least some corporations—come within the term "persons" as it is used in the Religious Freedom Restoration Act.

- Corporations can sue;
- Corporations can be sued;
- Corporations issue shares of stock which are units of ownership;
- In most of the cases in your casebook, the corporation's owners, called "shareholders" by some state statutes, called "stockholders" by others, do not run the corporation themselves; instead, they elect directors and the board of directors is responsible for management of the corporation;
- And, most important, a corporation's owners are generally not personally liable for the corporation's debt.

Whatever a corporation is—a person or an entity—it is what it is because of state statutes. Every state has enacted its own corporation statute that provides for the (1) creation of corporations and (2) the legal attributes of corporations created in that state.

2. What Is the State of Incorporation?

Each state's corporation statute is different from the corporation statutes in other states. This is important because a business can choose to incorporate in any state, even a state in which it has no business activities.

Assume, for example, that all of Bubba's Burritos Corporation's (BBC's) stockholders, directors and officers live in New York. None of them has ever even left New York, or has an idea about or interest in what happens beyond New York. And, BBC's business operations are in New York only.

Nonetheless, the people forming the BBC corporation can choose to incorporate it in a state other than New York, such as Delaware. And, if BBC incorporates in Delaware or any state other than New York that will be legally important.

3. What Is the Legal Importance of State of Incorporation?

3.1. How Is a "Foreign Corporation" Different from a "Domestic Corporation"?

State of incorporation is important first in that there are legal "hoops" that a corporation must "jump" through in order to do business in states other than its state of incorporation. If BBC is incorporated in Delaware (i.e., a "Delaware Corporation"), BBC will have to qualify to do business in New York as a "foreign corporation," even though all of its shareholders, directors, and business operations are in New York.

In New York, a corporation incorporated in New York is a "domestic corporation." A corporation in New York that was incorporated under the laws of Delaware, or any other state, is a "foreign corporation." New York and every other state require "foreign corporations" transacting business in the state to "qualify."

Qualification usually includes (i) obtaining authorization from the appropriate state agency, (ii) appointing a registered agent in that state, (iii) filing annual statements in that state, and (iv) paying fees and franchise taxes to that state. Corporations also pay fees to their state of incorporation, Thus, a New York based business that choses to incorporate in Delaware must pay fees to both New York and Delaware.

Most corporations transact business in a single state. Most such corporations incorporate in that state to avoid the complications and costs of having to qualify as a "foreign corporation."

3.2. *What Is the Importance of the "Internal Affairs" Doctrine?*

A New York based business that choses to incorporate in Delaware makes that choice to trigger the "internal affairs doctrine." The internal affairs doctrine is a conflicts of law rule that corporate governance matters are to be controlled by the laws of the state of incorporation. It is important to that you understand the internal affairs doctrine.

If, for example, BBC incorporates in Delaware, Delaware law will govern issues such as shareholders' right to vote, the procedures by which the board of directors act, and the duties of directors to the corporation. Again, this is true even though none of BBC's shareholders, directors, or burritos has ever been in Delaware.

Corporations that are incorporated in Delaware are commonly referred to as Delaware corporations. Corporations that incorporate in New York are commonly referred to as . . .

4. Why Do People Starting Businesses Choose to Incorporate in Delaware?

I have used Delaware as the state of incorporation in my hypotheticals because most large corporations—the kind of businesses that can afford to litigate and appeal and be involved in cases that appear in BA/BO casebooks—have incorporated in Delaware. In part, Delaware's popularity is a "chicken and egg" kind of thing.

Because more large businesses have incorporated in Delaware through the years, there is more case law interpreting the Delaware

General Corporation Law, which allows lawyers for a Delaware corporation to answer legal questions about that corporation with greater certainty than if the corporation was a New York corporation. That is important. What is probably more important to the people that decide whether to incorporate in Delaware is that Delaware's corporate law is generally sympathetic to a corporation's decision makers.

Because most professors teach at least certain provision of the Delaware corporate code, this book also teaches those provisions of the Delaware corporate code. And, because most professors also teach the Model Business Corporations Act (MBCA), this book teaches MBCA.

Most states have modeled their statutes in some measure on some version of the Model Business Corporation Act (MBCA). There have been several MBCA revisions. Most professors use a statutory supplement that includes MBCA(2016) and so my MBCA references are to MBCA(2016).

The MBCA is, in several exam-important places, different from the Delaware corporate code. I will flag those places as we come to them.

5. What Is the Importance of Federal Statutes in a Business Associations/Business Organizations Course?

There is no general federal corporation statute. There are, however, important federal statutes that govern certain corporate activities.

The most important such federal statute is the Internal Revenue Code. Most BA/BO professor is leaving that statute for your school's tax courses. If you drew a short straw. Here is what you need to know.

The earnings of most corporations are subject to what you need to call "double taxation." First, the corporation itself pays taxes on its earnings. Then, second, the shareholders of the corporation who receive their share of such earnings as dividends also pay tax on those same corporate earnings.

Later chapters will discuss briefly some of the federal securities statutes that apply to sales of stock and to tender offers and other corporate activities. Otherwise, corporate tax and securities regulation are left to advanced courses that are generally called "Corporate Taxation" and "Securities Regulations" and "Mergers and Acquisitions."

CHAPTER 12

What You Need to Know About Starting a Corporation

Exam questions about corporations may begin before the corporation is created. More specifically, watch for a question set in the days before the corporation exists—a fact pattern in which a person contracts on behalf of a corporation that does not yet exist, a pre-incorporation contract.

1. Who Are Promoters and What Legal Problems Do They Create?

For example, Larry, Moe, and Curly are planning to open a barbecue restaurant as a corporation, Bubba's Barbecue Corp (BBC). They want to be sure that they can lease the desired space from T before incurring the expense of forming a corporation. Accordingly, Moe signs a lease with T on behalf of BBC, a not yet existing corporation.

If such a hypothetical is on your exam, here is what you need to know:

(1) Moe is called a "promoter", i.e., a person who contracts on behalf of a corporation that does not yet exist;

(2) Promoters are personally liable on such contracts, even if they sign the contract on behalf of the not yet existing corporation;

(3) Promoters are not agents. Recall that an agent acts on behalf of a principal. Even principled promoters have no principals, since they are acting on behalf of a corporation that does not yet exist;

(4) The corporation is not liable on the contract until it ratifies the contract;

(5) Promoters remain personally liable on the contracts even after the corporation is formed and ratifies the contract. Promoters are relieved from liability only when the other party to the contract so agrees.

Larry, Moe and Curly might also decide that they need additional committed investors before they incur the expenses of creating a corporation. And so they persuade Shemp to offer to buy BBC stock when it is incorporated.

Shemp has made an offer—not a contract. It can't be a contract between Shemp and the corporation—the corporation does not yet exist. Under common law, offers are freely revocable. The MBCA calls Shemp's offer to buy stock in a corporation a "subscription" and makes a pre-incorporation subscription offers irrevocable for six months unless otherwise provided.

2. What Is Required to Create a Corporation?

A corporation is created, i.e., incorporated by sending a filing fee and a document to the appropriate state official. The MBCA calls that document "articles of incorporation." Delaware calls it "certificate of incorporation" in its statutes, but some courts applying the Delaware statute use the term "articles." Most professors use the term "articles" most often, and so will this book.

The person who files that document is called the "incorporator." All that is exam-important about the "incorporator" is that you not confuse the incorporator (who is not in any way important) with the promoter (who is important in pre-incorporation contracts).

What is more likely to be exam-important is information in the fact pattern about the contents of the articles. In most states, very little information is required to be included in the articles.

Delaware General Corporation Law section 102(a) requires only six items:

(1) name of the corporation;

(2) name and address of registered agent and address of the registered office;

(3) nature of the corporation's business which can be "to engage in any lawful act or activity";

(4) information about the corporation stock, including information about "classes of stock";

(5) name and address of the incorporator;

(6) names and addresses of initial directors.

Delaware General Corporation Law section 102(b) then includes a longer list of information that can be included in articles of incorporation, and most corporations' articles include much more than the six items listed above.

3. What Are Classes of Stock?

Both the Delaware General Corporation Law and the MBCA use the term "classes of stock." All corporations issue stock. Most corporations do not have classes of stock.

Generally, all of the shares of stock issued by a corporation are the same. Each share carries one vote on matters that shareholders vote on. If a dividend is declared, it is allocated equally among shares. Similarly, if the corporation is dissolved and a surplus remains after the corporation's creditors have been paid, that surplus is allocated equally among the shares.

Saying the same thing another way, most corporations issue only one class of stock. That stock is called common. None of the shares of a corporation with only one class of stock is different from other shares.

It is possible for a corporation's articles of incorporation to provide for more than one class of stock. For example, the Acme Corp articles can provide for two classes of stock—Class A and Class B—with only Class B having voting rights.

What you are more likely to see on your exam is a corporation whose articles provide for multiple classes, with each class having different rights when dividends are declared or when the corporation's assets are liquidated. A class of stock that has such a right to be paid first is commonly referred to as "preferred." A class of stock that has no right of prior payment is commonly referred to as "common."

To illustrate, Baker Corp has issued 1000 shares of Class 1 and 20 shares of Class 2. Baker Corp's articles provide that Class 2 has a $5 liquidation preference. Baker Corp dissolves and has a $1,100 surplus. Each of the 200 shares of Class 2 would be paid $5 first—before anything is distributed to the Class 1 stock. Under these facts, a holder of a Class 2 stock would receive $5 for each share of Class 2 stock she owns, while a holder of Class 1 stock would receive $1 a share for each share of Class 1 stock she owns.

4. How Is "Ultra Vires" Tested and What Is It?

On the exam, watch for a fact pattern with articles of incorporation that state a narrow corporate purpose such as the following: "The purpose of Bubba's Barbecue Corp. (BBC) is to prepare and sell barbecue brisket—just like in Texas on butcher paper with white bread. No plates or silverware. No sauce. No vegetables. No Carolina shredded pork crap."

Then, if the fact pattern tells you that BBC sells vegetables or Carolina barbecue or. . ., you tell your professor that BBC is acting "*ultra vires.*" There are two exam-important consequences of a corporation's acting ultra vires: (1) members of the BBC board of directors are personally liable for any losses the corporation sustained as a result of the ultra vires activities and (2) a court, on request of a BBC shareholder, can enjoin ultra vires activities.

There is also an important "non-consequence" of ultra vires activities. A corporation cannot rescind or otherwise get out of contracts that it made by establishing that the contract was ultra vires.

Ultra vires is only important if an exam fact pattern includes language from the articles of incorporation that state a narrow purpose. If, as authorized by the Delaware General Corporation Law, the articles provide that the corporation can engage in any lawful activities, then there are no ultra vires issues. Similarly, under MBCA 3.01, a corporation can engage in any lawful activity unless the corporation's articles state a narrow purpose and so no ultra vires issues if the corporation's articles state a more narrow purpose.

5. What Is "Authorized Stock"?

Watch also for a fact pattern which uses the phrases "articles of incorporation" and "shares of stock" in the same paragraph. The information about stock that a corporation's articles must include is the number of shares that a corporation is authorized to issue.

There are two important vocabulary terms in that last sentence: "authorized," which refers to the number of shares that a corporation can sell, and "issue," which refers to a corporation's sale of its own shares.

If you understand those terms, then you understand that BBC's articles of incorporation might authorize the issuance of 1,000 shares and BBC's board of directors chooses to issue only 400 shares. And you understand further that if a holder of some of those outstanding 400 shares later sells her shares to someone else then that sale of stock by a shareholder is not an issuance. You will later learn some concepts such as par value and preemptive rights that apply to a corporation's issuance of its own stock but not to stock transfers by shareholders.

Now if, in the prior paragraph, BBC has 400 shares outstanding and wants to issue an additional 900 shares there is a problem, because the BBC articles in the preceding paragraph only authorize BBC's issuance of 1,000. BBC can fix that problem by amending its articles.

We will learn (actually "you will learn"—I already know this stuff) more about amending articles in Chapter 15 and more about issuing stock in Chapter 14. For now, you need to learn four more vocabulary terms relevant to formation of a corporation: (1) de jure corporation, (2) de facto corporation, (3) corporation by estoppel, and (4) bylaws.

6. What Is a "De Jure Corporation"?

"De jure corporation" is a vocabulary term and nothing more. "De jure corporation" describes the corporation that exists because everything was done right: articles with the right information filed in the right place with the right filing fee. Your professor cannot base an exam question on a fact pattern in which everything was done right.

7. What Is a "De Facto Corporation"?

The terms "de facto corporation" and "corporation by estoppel" are used when (i) there were problems with the formation of the corporation, and (ii) people starting the business were unaware of the problems, and (iii) the business made a contract or commits a tort. The owners of this business will be personally liable for this contract or tort unless they can convince the court to apply either the de facto corporation doctrine or the corporation by estoppel doctrine.

The critical facts for de facto corporation are that the people running the business (1) attempted to incorporate and (2) thought the attempt was successful. For example, Larry, Moe, and Curly hire attorney James M. McGill to prepare and file articles of incorporation for BBC. They execute the articles and issue a check for the filing fee. McGill slips up by not filing the articles. Not knowing about McGill's slip, Larry, Moe, and Curly start operating BBC and contract to sell barbecue to Acme Nursing Home (Acme). They breach the contract with Acme.

Larry, Moe, and Curly might be able to avoid personal liability on the Acme contract by invoking the de facto corporation doctrine.

Some courts might conclude that Larry, Moe, and Curly did everything to form a corporation that we can reasonably expect them to do and so should be treated as if BBC was a de facto corporation.

8. What Is Corporation by Estoppel?

Larry, Moe, and Curly might also avoid personal contract liability by invoking corporation by estoppel. Then the critical fact will be whether Acme believed that it was contracting with a corporation. If Acme believed that BBC was a corporation, then Acme was willing to make a deal in which Larry, Moe, and Curly had no personal liability. If Acme was now permitted to recover from the personal assets of Larry, Moe, and Curly, Acme would be getting legal rights that it did not bargain for—an unfair "windfall."

In sum, a de facto corporation or corporation by estoppel, like a de jure corporation, protects a business's owners from personal liability on the business's obligations.

9. What Do You Need to Know About Bylaws?

While a de jure corporation is formed when the articles of incorporation are filed, MBCA and other corporate statutes also require that a corporation have not only articles of incorporation but also have bylaws. Bylaws establish the rules for corporate governance—matters such as titles and duties of officers and quorum requirements for board of director meetings and shareholder meetings.

Here are the four most important things for you to know about bylaws:

(1) A corporation's failure to adopt bylaws does not affect the corporation's de jure status.

(2) Bylaws, unlike articles, are not filed by the corporation with the state.

(3) A corporation's bylaw that is inconsistent with that corporation's articles of incorporation is invalid.

(4) The law with respect to amendment of bylaws is a mess.

In the unlikely event that your professor covered amendment of bylaws in class, you need to know more about the law with respect to amendment of bylaws than that it is a mess.

Originally, only shareholders could amend bylaws. MBCA 10.20 permits either the shareholders or board of directors to amend the bylaws unless articles give that power solely to shareholders.

You will later learn that an amendment to the articles must be approved by both the board of directors and the shareholders. So, it is easier to amend bylaws than articles. Shareholders can amend bylaws without board of director approval, unless the articles of incorporation otherwise provide.

To review, while it easy to start a corporation, starting a partnership is easier. If two or more people simply start a business together as co-owners without filing any papers with anybody, they are partners and their business is a partnership. That business can be a corporation only if they file the right papers (articles of incorporation) with the right filing fee in the right state office.

Think about why a public filing is required for corporations but not for partnerships. Remember the different legal attributes of partnerships and corporations?

If T contracts with Moe acting on behalf of BBP partnership, T does not need public notice that BBP is a partnership. BBP's status as a partnership does not affect T's rights to enforce that contract against the owners of the business.

On the other hand, if T contracts with Moe acting on behalf of BBC corporation, T should have at least public notice that BBC is a corporation. BBC's status as a corporation does affect T's rights to enforce that contract against the owners of the business. Thus, a filing is required to give public notice of the creation of a corporation and no filing is required to give public notice of the creation of a partnership.

CHAPTER 13

What You Need to Know About Who Is Liable for a Corporation's Debts

In general, there are five things that you need to know to answer an exam question about who is liable for a corporation's debts.

General "thing" 1: A corporation itself is liable for its debts. McDonald's Corporation is liable for its debts. Just be sure that the debt is indeed the corporation's debt.

General "thing" 2: Ignore statements in other student guides about a shareholder's "limited liability." Such statements are misleading at best. A shareholder does not have "limited liability" to a corporation's creditors. Instead, a shareholder has "limited loss exposure."

If you bought BBC stock for $100 and BBC closes owing creditors hundreds of thousands of dollars, you do not owe BBC creditors anything—not even $100. You lose your $100 investment. That is your limited loss exposure.

You do not owe BBC's creditors $100 just because you paid $100 for your stock. A shareholder's does not have liability to the corporation's creditors based on the amount she paid for her stock. Limited loss exposure, not limited liability.

General "thing" 3: A shareholder is not liable for the debts of a corporation. If you bought a share of McDonald's stock for $100, you have no liability to McDonald's creditors, absent special facts.

General "thing" 4: Use the phrase "piercing the corporate veil" in discussing whether there are special facts that support holding a shareholder personally liable for the corporation's debts.

General "thing" 5: Use the phrase "enterprise liability" in determining whether there are special facts that support holding the corporations owned by the same shareholder liable for each other's debts.

Now you need to integrate those five things with things previously covered. In other words, more review.

1. How Does a Corporation Become Indebted to Third Parties?

A corporation itself cannot incur debts. It is not McDonald's Corporation that makes contracts and commits torts for which McDonald's Corporation is liable. Rather, it is the contracts and torts of McDonald's Corporation's agents that creates liability for McDonald's Corporation consistent with the rules of agency law that you learned (or need to learn) in Part 1 of this book.

2. Who Is Liable for a Corporation's Debts to Third Parties?

More review. You know that a corporation is a legal entity and as such is liable for its own debts and owns property that can be a source for satisfying its debts. You also know from the bullet points of legal attributes of a corporation in Chapter 11 that, "a corporation's owners—called 'shareholders' by some state statutes, called 'stockholders' by others—are *generally* not personally liable for the corporation's debt." Note that "weasel word" "generally."

You don't find that qualifier in corporate statutes. MBCA 6.22(b) is typical: "A shareholder of a corporation is not liable for any liabilities of the corporation. . . ."

You do find the qualifier "generally" in case law. Especially in cases that use the phrase "piercing the corporate veil." And so you need to know about piercing the corporate veil when you encounter an exam fact pattern in which a creditor of a corporation is trying to hold one or more of that corporation's shareholders liable for a debt owed by the corporation.

3. What Are the Eight Things That You Need to Know About Piercing the Corporate Veil?

Here are the eight exam-important things that you need to know about piercing the corporate veil:

(1) As the prior sentence states, piercing the corporate veil imposes liability on one or more shareholders. If Larry, Moe, and Curly are the shareholders of BBC, a court can pierce the corporate veil as to all shareholders or only some shareholders.

(2) Piercing the corporate veil is a court-created concept.

(3) While courts can pierce the corporate veil, they are reluctant to do so. Rarely happens. Remember protection of the corporation's owners from liability for the corporation's debts is an essential legal attribute of corporations. Remember corporate

statutes provide that protection with no statutory exceptions.

(4) There are no "leading cases" on piercing the corporate veil. The cases that will be important on your exam are the cases that your professor assigned.

(5) There are no general rules that can be derived from the cases. The cases are fact-specific. You need to be prepared to compare the facts of the cases your professor assigned to the facts in your professor's exam question.

(6) There can be corporations with only one shareholder. And that shareholder can itself be a corporation. The fact that a corporation has only one shareholder is not itself a basis for piercing the corporate veil.

(7) The number of shareholders is a relevant but unmentioned fact. None of the piercing the corporate veil cases in casebooks involve a corporation with more than ten shareholders. None of the cases mention that fact.

(8) Instead cases (i) mention five, ten or more other factors and (ii) emphasize that no one fact is determinative and (iii) explain that the decision is based on the "totality of the circumstances." Factors commonly mentioned by these cases in discussing veil piercing include:

(i) failure to observe corporate formalities;

(ii) shareholder's treating the funds and other assets of the corporation as her own;

(iii) undercapitalization.

Examples of (i) non-observance of corporate formalities include failure to hold directors' meetings, failure to hold shareholders' meetings, and failure to prepare and preserve minutes of such meetings. It is hard to see how that affects creditors of the corporation. And harder to see why that should enable creditors of the corporation to recover the corporation's debts from a shareholder.

Nonetheless you will see failure to observe corporate formalities discussed in the piercing the corporate veil cases your professor assigned. And so, your professor will want to see that mentioned, if not discussed, in your essay answer.

It is easier to see the relevance of factor (ii), a shareholder's treating the funds and other assets of the corporation as her own, in piercing the corporate veil. If a shareholder does not treat the corporation as a separate entity, why should that shareholder be able to escape liability by asserting that the corporation's creditors, must treat the corporation as a separate entity? Your prof might have used the term "alter ego doctrine" in discussing this second factor.

(iii) Undercapitalization means something more than the corporation is unable to pay that creditor who is arguing that the corporate veil be pierced. If the corporation were able to pay this creditor at the time of the suit, the creditor would not have to be arguing that the corporate veil be pierced.

In determining whether to pierce the corporate veil because the corporation is undercapitalized, the court compares the resources of the corporation (including liability insurance) and its possible liability risks. Adequacy of capital for a corporation that makes air bags for BMW will be different from adequacy of capital for a corporation that makes paper bags for WaWa. Some professors have argued that adequacy of capital should be the critical factor in determining whether a court should pierce.

And, at least some professors argue that undercapitalization should be more important in piercing the corporate veil to benefit a tort victim, than in piercing the corporate veil to benefit a contract claimant. A contract claimant has a pre-contract opportunity to determine whether a corporation has sufficient assets before entering into a contract. A tort victim does not have a similar pre-tort opportunity to determine whether a corporation has sufficient assets. While reported cases do not make this distinction, if your professor does, then it is at least worth mentioning on your exam.

Also worth mentioning on your exam are the words "parent corporation" and "subsidiary corporation." Particularly when facts are that one corporation—the parent—owns at least half of the stock of another corporation—the subsidiary. That fact alone does not justify piercing the corporate veil so as to hold the parent liable for the debts of the subsidiary.

Instead, treat questions about piercing the corporate veil so as to hold a shareholder that is a corporation liable no different from questions about piercing the corporate veil so as to hold an individual liable. Use the same "totality of the circumstances" approach.

4. How Is Enterprise Liability Both Similar to and Different from Piercing the Corporate Veil?

What is different are questions of the liability exposure of multiple corporations owned by the same person—brother/sister corporations. There is some authority for the theory that if two or more corporations are owned by the same shareholder, or shareholders, and are operated as a single enterprise, then all of the assets of all of the corporations in this enterprise should be available to satisfy the claim of a creditor of any one of the corporations that is a part of the enterprise. This theory is cleverly called "enterprise liability."

Assume, for example, that (i) C is a creditor of B Corp, (ii) Moe owns all of the stock of B Corp and S Corp, and (iii) the two corporations use each other's assets. C is unable to collect the debt owed by B Corp from the assets of B Corp. If C can convince the court to apply enterprise liability, C will be able to collect its debt owed by B Corp from the assets of the related corporation S Corp.

Let's be sure that you understand both the difference and the similarities of piercing the corporate veil and enterprise liability.

First, the difference. Piercing the corporate veil can be invoked by a creditor of B Corp to hold shareholder Moe liable for the debts of B Corp. Alternatively, enterprise liability can be invoked by a creditor of B Corp to hold sister corporation C Corp liable for the debts of B Corp.

Now, the similarities. In both piercing the corporate veil and enterprise liability, the plaintiff creditor is able to recover its debts from a defendant who was not its debtor because the defendant failed to treat the debtor corporation as a separate legal entity. Both piercing the corporate veil and enterprise liability are fact specific and depend on the totality of the circumstances.

CHAPTER 14

What You Need to Know About a Corporation's Issuance of Stock

Vocabulary is a big part of an answer to an essay question on a corporation's issuance of stock. Starting with the word "issuance."

1. What Is an Issuance of Stock?

An issuance of stock is a form of sale of stock. More specifically, an issuance of stock occurs when a corporation sells its own stock.

Only a corporation can issue its own stock. And the corporation can only issue the number of shares authorized in the articles. Subject to that limit, the board of directors decides the number of shares the corporation issues.

2. What Is the Difference Between Authorized Stock and Issued Stock?

Even though the articles authorize the issuance of 100,000 shares, the board of directors might decide to only issue 500 shares.

In that example, there are 100,000 authorized shares but only 500 outstanding shares.

The board of directors also decides the form and the amount of consideration the corporation receives in exchange for the stock and to whom the corporation issues stock. Ordinarily, a corporation issues stock for money, but Delaware, the MBCA, and most states' corporate statutes also permit stock to be issued for property, services rendered, services to be rendered, or a promissory note. A few states still adhere to historical limitations and do not permit issuance of stock for promissory notes or future services.

When stock is issued for property, services, or any consideration other than cash, the board of directors also decides what the value of the consideration is. If BBC is issuing 50 shares of stock to Moe in exchange for Redacre, the board of directors decides on the value of Redacre. If the Board of directors decides that the value of Redacre received in exchange for its stock is $1,000, then BBC's balance sheet would show a $1,000 increase in BBC's assets and a $1,000 increase in BBC's equity.

BBC's board of directors' valuation of the consideration received for the issuance of 50 shares of BBC stock is legally significant if the BBC stock is "par value" stock. Stock is "par value" stock only if the articles so provide.

3. What Is "Par Value"?

A corporation's articles of incorporation can provide not only the number of authorized shares but also the characteristics of the stock. One possible characteristic of stock is "par value."

Par value is the minimum price for which stock may be issued if the corporation's articles provide a par value for its shares. Notice the limiting words "minimum" and "issued." If BBC's articles provide that its stock has a par value of $7 a share, then BBC could not issue a share of stock for less than $7 in cash or for other consideration worth less than $7.

Par value has no effect on the price for which a BBC shareholder later resells their shares. Moe could, in our example, later sell his $7 par BBC stock to Shemp or anyone else for less than $7 a share or more than $7 a share.

Because par value is merely the minimum issuance price, BBC could issue shares of $7 par stock for consideration with a value of more than $7 a share. Thus, in our hypothetical, BBC could issue only 50 shares of $7 par stock to Moe for Redacre, even though the BBC board of directors determine that Redacre was worth $1,000.

Par value stock issued for consideration with a value less than par is called "watered stock." The members of the board of directors that authorized the issuance are personally liable to the corporation for the amount of the "water," as is the buyer.

If, for example, the BBC board of directors issued 1,000 shares of $7 par stock to Byer for Redacre and it is later determined that the value of Redacre at the time of the issuance was only $2,000, then there is $5,000 of water. The corporation can recover that $5,000 from the BBC board of directors or from Byer.

To review, the general rule is that the board of directors determines the price at which the corporation issues its own stock. The "exception" to that rule is that the price determined by the board must be at least the par value if the articles of incorporation provide a par value.

And, articles of incorporation that provide a par value for shares is the exception. You are more likely to see "par value" on your professor's exam than in your corporate clients' articles.

4. What Is Dilution?

A corporation issues stock not only at the time it is formed, but also thereafter to obtain additional funding. If BBC, an existing corporation, needs additional funds to expand, one way of obtaining the needed additional funds is to issue additional shares. Such subsequent issuances can raise dilution problems.

Dilution can most easily be explained by illustration. Assume that Shemp owns 60 of the 100 shares BBC has issued. As the owner of 60% of BBC's outstanding shares, Shemp has significant influence over BBC. If BBC later issues 300 shares to other people, Shemp's voting influence has been diluted.

The price determined by the BBC board for any such subsequent stock issue can result in an economic dilution of the economic interests of the existing shareholders. If a corporation issues new shares for consideration that is less than the worth of the existing stock, the result is economic dilution.

Assume for example that BBC has a net worth of $100,000 and has 100 shares outstanding. Moe owns 50 of the 100 shares—50% of the outstanding BBC stock. Moe's stock is worth $50,000 or $1,000 a share—$50,000/50. If the BBC board of directors later issues 100 shares to Shemp for $500 a share, then the value of Moe's shares have been economically diluted from $1,000 shares to $750 a share ([$100,000 + $50,000]/[100,000 + 100,000]).

5. What Are Preemptive Rights?

Preemptive rights provide one form of protection for existing shareholders from dilution. Preemptive rights enable a shareholder to maintain their percentage of ownership when the corporation issues additional stock.

To illustrate, Moe owns 50% of the outstanding stock of BBC. If the board of directors later decide to issue 1,000 shares for $50 a share, then Moe has the opportunity (but not the obligation) to buy 500 of the 1,000 new shares at $50 a share.

Under the MBCA and the Delaware Corporate Code, a shareholder has preemptive rights only if the articles of incorporation expressly so provide. And, even if the articles of incorporation expressly provide for preemptive rights, they do not apply to the issuance of stock for consideration other than cash.

Suppose that BBC needs Redacre and the owner of Redacre is only willing to sell Redacre for BBC stock. If BBC's shareholders are able to exercise preemptive rights, then BBC may not be able to obtain Redacre.

To summarize, preemptive rights protect a shareholder from economic dilution by the board of directors' issuing stock for less than its fair market value only if (i) the corporation's articles provide for preemptive rights, and (ii) the corporation's board of directors is issuing the stock for cash.

What usually protects existing shareholders from the economic dilution resulting from the board of directors' issuing additional shares at an inadequate price is the fact that directors are often also substantial shareholders. This protection can be less than complete in situations in which the persons to whom the stock is being issued for a less than adequate price are directors themselves.

If you encounter such a situation on your BA/BO final exam, discuss the directors' fiduciary duties to the corporation. Chapter 17 discusses the directors' fiduciary duties to the corporation. To foreshadow (without overshadowing) that discussion, in "interested director transactions," such as a director purchasing shares from the corporation, the general rule is that the transaction must either (i) be approved by disinterested directors or shareholders or (ii) the buying director must prove that the transaction was fair to the corporation.

CHAPTER 15

What You Need to Know About the Role of Shareholders in Running a Corporation

Under the standard model of corporate governance, shareholders do not run a corporation. As we will see in Chapter 16, under the standard model of corporate governance, the board of directors runs a corporation.

The primary corporate governance role of shareholders is to elect the members of the board of directors who will have the ultimate responsibility for running the corporation. Accordingly, the one word answer to the question "what is the role of shareholder in running a corporation" is "vote."

But that one word is too short an answer. In answering exam questions about the role of shareholders in running a corporation, you might also need to know about:

(1) shareholders' right to inspect corporate records for a proper purpose;

(2) annual meetings and special meetings;

(3) quorums, majorities, and pluralities;

(4) record owner on record date;

(5) proxy;

(6) straight and cumulative voting in electing directors;

(7) voting trusts and voting agreements.

1. When Can Shareholders Inspect Corporate Records?

Since informed shareholders are more likely to vote intelligently, it would seem that shareholders should have the right to inspect corporate records. And they do. Both common law and most corporate statutes recognize shareholders' rights to gain information by inspecting corporate records.

The issue in shareholder information rights fact patterns is typically whether the shareholder has a "proper purpose." A proper purpose is one that is related to a role that shareholders play.

Obtaining information about the identity of, and addresses for, other shareholders in order to urge other shareholders to vote for Shemp for director is a proper purpose. Obtaining the same information to urge other shareholders to vote for Donald Trump or Joe Biden for President is not.

Exam fact patterns focusing on shareholders' voting typically involve a combination of the following three questions:

1. When do shareholders vote?
2. Who votes?
3. How do shareholders vote?

2. When Do Shareholders Vote?

Shareholders vote at shareholder meetings. Since typically directors are elected each year, shareholders meet each year to vote on directors. Such meetings are called annual meetings of shareholders. Not all of corporation law is complicated.

Additionally, shareholders might be called to a special meeting to vote on certain corporate matters such as amendments to the articles of incorporation, mergers, sales of substantially all of the assets, or dissolution. These corporate actions requiring shareholder approval are commonly referred to as "fundamental corporate changes." You will learn about these fundamental corporate changes in Chapter 23.

For now, understand the difference between the shareholders' role in voting on directors and the shareholders' role in voting on amendments, mergers, sales, or dissolution. When shareholders vote on directors, they are deciding who the directors will be. Shareholders get to make that decision.

Shareholders don't get to decide whether to amend the articles or merge or sell assets or dissolve. Rather, when shareholders' vote on amendments to the articles, mergers, sales of assets, or dissolution, they are merely voting on whether to approve decisions made by the board of directors to amend, to merge, to sell or to dissolve.

Not much to this question of when do shareholders vote.

3. When Shareholders Vote, Who Has the Right to Vote?

Your understanding of the second possible shareholder voting question—who votes—needs to be more complete. Remember that a corporation's articles of incorporation can provide for more than one class of stock and that the different classes can have different voting rights. For example, the BBC articles could provide for Class A stock with general voting rights, Class B stock with the right to vote only on mergers, and Class C with no voting rights.

3.1. What Is the "Record Owner as of the Record Date"?

Harder to understand is the concept of "record owner as of the record date." This concept is based on the premise that a corporation keeps records as to who its shareholders are and provides information to these shareholders of record in advance of any meeting of shareholders.

A corporation like BBC, with relatively few shareholders and relatively few transactions in its shares, will probably actually have records with the name of its actual shareholders. For a publicly traded corporation like McDonald's, a "street name registration" is used.

Most people do not own stock in a specific company. Most people own stock through their 401(k) program, which only allows them to own mutual funds. Most people own shares of Vanguard, not McDonalds.

If you own McDonald's stock, your McDonald's shares are probably held in an account at a brokerage firm, bank, broker-dealer, or other similar organization. The organization holding your account is considered the shareholder of record for purposes of voting at shareholder meetings. You have the right to instruct that organization on how to vote the shares held in your account.

People shown on the corporate records as owning stock are the "record owners." "Record date" is a date set by the board of directors in advance of the meeting that serves as a cutoff point. This gap period between the record date and the vote gives the corporation time to determine who is entitled to vote and send proper notices and information to those entitled to vote.

To illustrate, assume that BBC's annual shareholders meeting date is April 5 and that the BBC board of directors establishes March 4th as the record date. If the BBC share transfer records as of March 4th show that Moe owns 100 shares of BBC stock, then Moe would be able to vote the 100 shares of BBC at April 5. And, if Moe sold those shares to Shemp on April 1, Moe would still be the person to vote the shares at the April 5th meeting. Even though Moe does not own the shares as of the date of the vote, Moe still gets to vote since he is still the record owner as of the record date.

3.2. *What Is a "Proxy," and How Much of the Law Relating to Proxies Is Covered in a Basic Business Associations/Business Organizations Course?*

In our last hypothetical, Shemp can gain the right to vote by obtaining a proxy from Moe. A record shareholder can authorize someone else to vote their shares. The word "proxy" is used both to describe that authorization and to identify the person so authorized. That person is also referred to as the proxy holder.

There are four things that you need to know about the state law relating to proxies. First, a proxy is effective for eleven months unless the proxy states otherwise. Second, a proxy is revocable by the record shareholder even if the proxy states it is irrevocable. Third, a proxy is irrevocable only if it both states that it is irrevocable and is also "coupled with an interest." Fourth, "coupled with an interest" means that the proxy holder has some interest in the stock other than just voting the shares.

If Moe sells his shares to Shemp after the record date, but before the shareholder meeting, and grants Shemp an irrevocable proxy, that proxy would be coupled with an interest and so would indeed be irrevocable. A proxy holder like Shemp—a person who bought the shares after the record date—is the most frequently tested example of proxy holder coupled with an interest.

There is also a substantial body of federal law governing proxies that will be considered in Chapter 22. The remainder of this chapter covers the question how do shareholders vote.

4. How Do Shareholders Vote?

4.1. How Is a Quorum Determined?

Shareholders, like other groups, cannot act without a quorum. With shareholders, however, unlike other groups, a quorum is not determined by how many people are present. Don't count noses. Count shares instead. A quorum and the vote required are determined by considering the number of shares and not the number of shareholders.

Assume that BBC has 1,000 outstanding shares and 11 shareholders. Moe, one of the 11 shareholders, owns 600 of the outstanding share. Moe alone is the quorum unless BBC's articles of incorporation require a supermajority such as 2/3 of the outstanding shares as the quorum. The existence of a quorum is a possible issue in any exam fact pattern about how shareholders vote.

With respect to the number of votes required for shareholder action or approval, the focus is again on the number of shares, not the number of shareholders. A shareholder with 600 shares has six times as many votes as the person with 100 shares.

With respect to the number of votes required for the most frequently tested shareholder vote—election of directors, you need to focus on the relevant statutory language.

First, the statutory word "plurality." Both the Delaware and MBCA statutory provisions on election of directors use the term "plurality." If Larry gets 100 votes, Curly gets 101 votes and Moe gets 102 votes, Moe wins. No one has a majority but Moe has the necessary plurality.

4.2. *What Is Cumulative Voting?*

Now (second), the statutory phrase "cumulative voting." Both the Delaware and MBCA provisions on the election and removal of directors use the term "cumulative voting," and both Delaware and the MBCA make cumulative voting available in shareholders' election or removal of directors only if a corporation's articles expressly provide for "cumulative voting."

Cumulative voting can best be explained by illustrations showing the difference between "cumulative voting" and "straight voting."

Assume that BBC has 300 shares outstanding and a three-person board of directors. Moe owns 100 shares; Curly owns 99 shares; Larry owns 98 shares; and Shemp owns 3 shares. Each of the shareholders has three adult children. Each of the shareholders wants their three children to be directors and votes for their children.

And, assume that the BBC articles do not provide for cumulative voting. "Straight voting" is the term commonly used to describe shareholders' voting for directors where the articles do not provide for cumulative voting.

With straight voting, each director position is filled by a separate shareholder vote. If, as in our example, there are three expiring positions on the board, there will be three elections at the meeting—one for each vacant seat on the board. Unless the articles otherwise provide, each shareholder will cast one vote for each share they hold and will do so in each of the three elections.

Think about what is likely to happen in our illustration. In the vote on the first board seat, Moe casts his 100 votes for his child,

Curly casts his 99 votes for his child, Larry casts his 98 votes for his child, and Shemp does not even bother to vote. No candidate gets a majority. Nonetheless, Moe's child wins the first board seat because Moe's child has the necessary plurality.

And the result will be the same in the other two shareholder votes on BBC directors. Moe has the needed plurality and so Moe can elect Moe's three children as the three directors. The shareholder with the most shares can elect all of the directors unless there is either cumulative voting or some form of voting agreement involving two or more of the shareholders.

Let's do cumulative voting first. It is an exam favorite.

You already know three things about cumulative voting: (1) it is relevant to shareholder's vote for directors, (2) it is only relevant if the corporation's articles of incorporation expressly provide for cumulative voting, and (3) it is different from "straight voting."

Cumulative voting is different from straight voting in two important respects. First, with cumulative voting, there is a single "at-large" election. In the above BBC shareholder vote hypothetical, there would be one shareholder vote to elect three directors, instead of three separate votes. Second, cumulative voting means that (i) the number of votes that a shareholder can cast in that at-large election is determined by multiplying the number of directors to be elected by the number of shares he owns and (ii) the shareholder can cast all of his votes for one candidate.

Thus, in the BBC hypothetical, Moe has 300 total votes, Curly has 297 total votes and Larry has 293 votes and Shemp has 9 votes. Assuming that Moe, Curly, and Larry vote intelligently, each will be able to elect one of their children to the BBC board of directors.

The mathematics of voting intelligently under cumulative voting can be very complicated. I hope your professor understands that and does not expect you to be able to learn and apply a bunch of formulae. If you do not have such an understanding professor, then you need to understand the next paragraph about the "easiest" formula for determining the number of shares a shareholder needs to be sure that they can elect one director under cumulative voting.

The formula involves addition, division, and, worst of all, a fraction. The number of shares voting is the numerator (top part) of a fraction. The denominator (bottom part) of the fraction is the number of directors plus one. So if 1,000 shares are voting and three directors are to be elected, the fraction would be 1,000/(3+1) or 1,000/4. And, 1,000/4 is 250. To elect a director you need one share more than the number generated by the fraction—you need 251 shares. And, I hope that is more cumulative voting math than you need know for your BA/BO exam.

Cumulative voting gives shareholders, other than the shareholder with the largest number of shares, a voice in the management of a corporation. Remember, though, cumulative voting is available only if the articles so provide and, even then, only applies to the election of or removal of directors.

Shareholders can also gain a greater voice in the management of a corporation by agreeing to combine their voting powers. Reconsider the hypothetical in which Moe has 100 shares, Curly has 99 shares, Larry has 98 shares and Shemp has 3 shares. If Shemp and Larry agree to combine their votes, that combination has more votes than Moe.

When you encounter an exam fact pattern involving an agreement that controls shareholders' voting such as the above agreement between Shemp and Larry, you need to know whether (1) it is a voting trust or a voting agreement, (2) it complies with the requirements of the state corporation code, and (3) it is effective.

4.3. What Is a Voting Trust?

The term "voting trust" is descriptive, if not self-explanatory. If Shemp and Larry agree on a voting trust, they will:

(1) set up a trust;

(2) transfer their shares to the trust so that the trust is now the record owner of their shares and they are the beneficial owners;

(3) designate a person to serve as trustee and vote the shares held by the trust; and

(4) provide instructions in the trust agreement as to how the shares are to be voted.

State corporation statutes authorize shareholder voting trusts. Typically, the statutes require that the trust agreement be filed with the corporation.

A voting trust is a legally effective way for shareholders to combine their voting power. The trustee has a fiduciary duty to vote the shares as instructed in the trust instrument. If the trustee does not do so, a court will compel the trustee to vote the shares as instructed in the trust instrument.

Voting trusts are also complicated and cumbersome. Reconsider the four steps set out above.

What if Larry and Shemp simply agree to vote their shares the same way on certain matters? Such as an agreement between two or more shareholders is generally called a voting agreement.[1]

---

[1] If you have an "older" professor, your prof might use the older term "pooling agreement" instead.

4.4. How Is a Voting Agreement Different from a Voting Trust?

The voting agreement case that you need to know for your exam is the case involving a circus incorporated in Delaware, *Ringling Bros.-Barnum & Bailey Combined Shows v. Ringling*. There, two shareholders, Mrs. Ringling & Mrs. Haley, entered into agreement that they would both vote their shares for the same slate of directors. Mrs. Ringling complied with the agreement. Mrs. Haley breached. She voted for some, but not all, of the agreed upon slate of director candidates.

When Mrs. Ringling sued, Mrs. Haley contended that the agreement was invalid. At the time of the litigation, Delaware had a statutory provision authorizing voting trusts but no statutory provision regarding voting agreements. Nonetheless, the court upheld the validity of the agreement.

Since then, the Delaware Corporate Code and the MBCA have expressly recognized voting agreements. More importantly, the MBCA provision, but not the Delaware provision, expressly provides for specific performance. In other words, under the MBCA the court can compel the breaching party to vote as they agreed to do.

In the Delaware circus case, the court did not order specific performance. Instead, it held that the votes by Mrs. Haley that were in breach of the agreement should simply be disregarded. As a result, one of the directors who would have been elected had Mrs. Haley not breached was not elected.

Looking back, both voting trusts and voting agreements are legal. And both can affect how shareholders vote on all matters requiring a shareholder vote, not just the election of directors. The disadvantage of a voting trust, as compared to a voting agreement, is that a voting trust is a more formal, complicated arrangement requiring transfer of record ownership of the shares to a trust. The advantage of a voting trust as compared to a voting agreement is that a voting trust is always effective. Unless the corporation is incorporated in an MBCA state, the voting agreement might not be effective—might not be specifically enforceable.

Looking ahead, some people are both shareholders and directors. The law treats directors differently from shareholders, even when the same person is both a shareholder and a director. Directors cannot commit in advance to how they will vote or that they will pool their votes—unless there is an MBCA 7.32 shareholders agreement.

In the next chapter you will learn (or least be given the opportunity to learn) about 7.32 shareholders agreements and more about the differences between the roles of shareholders and the roles of the board of directors.

CHAPTER 16

What You Need to Know About the Role of Directors and Officers in Running a Corporation

In theory, corporate law separates ownership and control. Shareholders, whom we think of as owning the corporation, have no power to control a corporation's day to day operations or a corporation's long term policies. Shareholders simply vote for directors and some "fundamental corporate changes" mentioned in Chapter 15 and covered again later. The board of directors, not the shareholder/owners, runs the corporation.

1. What Do Corporate Statutes Provide About the Role of the Board of Directors?

Again, the board of directors runs the corporation. That is essentially what state corporate statutes say. The following provisions of the Delaware Corporate Code and the MBCA are representative:

DEL CODE § 141

(a) The business and affairs of every corporation organized under this chapter shall be managed by or under the direction of a board of directors, except as may be otherwise provided in this chapter or in its certificate of incorporation.

MBCA § 8.01

(b) Except as may be provided in an agreement authorized under section 7.32 . . . all corporate powers shall be exercised by or under the authority of the board of directors of the corporation, and the business and affairs of the corporation shall be managed by or under the direction, and subject to the oversight, of its board of directors.

2. What Do Corporate Statutes Provide About the Role of an Individual Director?

Note that the statutes refer to the "board of directors," not to directors. The statutes give the authority to run the corporation to the board as a group.

Directors can only act as a body. An individual director does not have the power to act on behalf of the corporation. The relationship between a director and the corporation is not an agency relationship. Directors are not agents of the corporation.

Notice also, both the Delaware and MBCA provisions use the phrase "under the direction of." This phrase authorizes the board of directors to delegate managerial functions to corporate officers and other corporate employees. Both the Delaware statute and the

MBCA contemplate that the board of directors will select and supervise the corporation's officers, who will then hire managers and others who will make the day to day operational decisions.

3. What Does a Board of Directors Actually Do?

This chapter began with the words "in theory" and has explained the theoretical decision-making model of the Delaware statute and the MBCA. You need to understand this statutory model, but you also need to understand what happens in the real world.

Think about the number of decisions that must be made each day in a large corporation like McDonald's. And think about the other responsibilities of the people serving on the McDonald's board of directors, which in 2025 includes the Chairman and Chief Executive Officer of Marriott. Inc. and the Commissioner of the Women's National Bankruptcy Association.

At McDonald's, corporate officers and other employees run the day to day operations of the corporation. Corporate officers and employees, unlike directors, are agents of the corporation. When you encounter an exam fact pattern involving officers, watch for Chapter 1 agency issues.

In a corporation with relatively few shareholders, such as Bubba's Barbecue Corporation (BBC), there is not any real separation of ownership and control. The owners control BBC's day to day operations and BBC's long term policies.

In both large, publicly held corporations like McDonald's and small, closely held corporations like BBC, a person can be (i) a shareholder, and (ii) a director and (iii) an officer. One person with three roles.

When you encounter such a person in a fact pattern, you need to be mindful in which role they are acting. The role and rules for a shareholder are different from the role and rules for a director.

4. Why Is It Important to Determine Whether a Person Who Is Both a Shareholder and a Director Is Acting in Her Role as Director or in Her Role as a Shareholder?

The baseball case, *McQuade v. Stoneham*, is the case that most BA/BO casebooks use to make that point. McGraw, McQuade and Stoneham, three of the shareholders of the National Exhibition Company, which owned the New York Giants, agreed that they would "use their best endeavors for the purpose of continuing as directors of said Company and as officers the following (followed by their three names)."

As a result of Stoneham's breach of this agreement, McQuade was voted out as treasurer. When McQuade sued, the New York Court of Appeals concluded that the agreement concerning the appointment of officers was illegal and void.

The court reasoned that (i) directors, not shareholders, appoint officers, (ii) when the three agreed to appoint each other as officers, they were agreeing as to what they would do as directors, and (iii) directors, unlike shareholders, are fiduciaries to the corporation and, as such, must exercise independent judgment. Accordingly, any such agreement as to what they would do as directors violated public policy.

The court in *McQuade v. Stoneham* also stated by way of dictum that the agreement about electing each other to the board was valid. When McGraw, McQuade, and Stoneham vote for directors, they are acting as shareholders, not as directors. And as you recall from Chapter 15, shareholders can enter into voting agreements.

Do you recall the reference to MBCA § 7.32 in MBCA § 8.01? It is an important provision—important enough for me to reproduce in part, and important enough for you to read carefully.

5. What Is a Shareholder Agreement (and Why Is It Being Covered in This Chapter on the Role of the Board of Directors)?

MBCA § 7.32 Shareholder Agreements

(a) An agreement among the shareholders of a corporation that complies with this section is effective among the shareholders and the corporation even though it is inconsistent with one or more other provisions of this Act in that it:

(1) eliminates the board of directors or restricts the discretion or powers of the board of directors;

* * *

(3) establishes who shall be directors or officers * * *

(b) An agreement authorized by this section shall be:

(1) set forth (i) in the articles of incorporation or bylaws and approved by all persons who are shareholders at the time of the agreement or (ii) in a written agreement that is signed by all persons who are shareholders at the time of the agreement and is made known to the corporation * * *

(c) Any purchaser of shares who, at the time of purchase, did not have any knowledge of the existence of the agreement, shall be entitled to the rescission of the purchase. A purchaser shall be deemed to have knowledge of the existence of the agreement if its existence is noted on the certificate * * *

(e) An agreement authorized by this section that limits the discretion or powers of the board of directors shall relieve the directors of, and impose upon the person or persons in whom such discretion or powers are vested, liability for acts or omissions imposed by law on directors to the extent that the discretion or powers of the directors are limited by the agreement. * * *

There are at least five things you need to take away from this excerpt of MBCA § 7.32:

(1) Agreements under MBCA § 7.32 are called "shareholder agreements."

(2) MBCA § 7.32 shareholder agreements must be agreed to by all the shareholders at the time of the agreements.

(3) In an MBCA § 7.32 agreement, all shareholders can agree to eliminate the board of directors so that shareholders are running the corporation or instructing the board as to what it can do or will do.

* * *

(5) MBCA § 7.32 shareholder agreements are different from the shareholder voting agreements considered in Chapter 15 in that:

   a. MBCA § 7.32 shareholder agreements affect how a corporation is governed; shareholder voting agreements simply affect how the contracting shareholders will vote their shares.

   b. MBCA § 7.32 shareholder agreements are valid only if all shareholders at the time of the agreement enter into the agreement; shareholder voting agreements require only that two or more shareholders agree.

(6) If an MBCA § 7.32 shareholder agreement eliminates the board of directors so that shareholders have the power of directors, those shareholders have the

same "liability for acts or omissions imposed by law on directors."

In the next chapter, you will learn about the liability for acts or omissions imposed by law on directors.

CHAPTER 17

What You Need to Know About the Legal Obligations of Directors to the Corporation

Watch for an exam fact pattern with the following two characteristics. First, a corporation has lost money (or lost an opportunity to make money). Second, that corporation's board of directors (or, equally likely, a particular director) did "tacky things," i.e., was arguably stupid, lazy, or greedy.

In dealing with these two facts, you will need to state and analyze possible arguments about the directors' legal obligations to the corporations. More specifically, you will need to deal with directors' duty of care and duty of loyalty.

1. What Is the Basis for the Legal Obligations of Directors to the Corporation?

You already know that an agent has a fiduciary duty to its principal. And, you already know that partners are agents, that officers of a corporation are agents of the corporation, but that directors are not agents of the corporation.

While directors are not agents, directors are fiduciaries. A fiduciary is someone who is acting in the interest of someone else. For example, a trustee acts on behalf of a beneficiary of the trust and owes a legal duty, i.e., a fiduciary duty, to the beneficiaries. Similarly, directors act on behalf of the corporation, and so directors are fiduciaries and owe a fiduciary duty to the corporation.

2. What Are the Three Primary Sources That Affect the Directors' Legal Obligations to the Corporation?

In answering an exam question about directors' legal obligations to the corporation, be prepared to discuss the three different sources that affect directors' legal obligations to the corporation: (1) the relevant state statute, (2) the corporation's articles of incorporation and (3) case law. The relevant state statute will be the corporation statute of the state of incorporation.

You already know the "internal affairs doctrine." The laws of the state of incorporation control matters arising from the relationship between the corporation and its directors and its shareholders. The legal obligations of directors to the corporation is an "internal affairs" matter.

If BBC is incorporated in Delaware, then look to the Delaware General Corporation Law and case law applying the Delaware General Corporation Law to determine the legal obligations of directors. If BBC is incorporated in an MBCA state, then look to the corporate code and case law applying the MBCA corporate code to determine the legal obligations of directors.

3. What Are the Primary Legal Obligations of Directors to a Corporation?

The two primary legal obligations of directors are (1) a duty of care and (2) a duty of loyalty. Cases applying the Delaware corporate law and cases applying the MBCA consistently discuss directors' duty of care and duty of loyalty. Thus, when you encounter an exam fact pattern with (1) a corporation that has lost money (or lost an opportunity to make more money), and (2) the corporation's board of directors (or, equally likely, a particular director) was arguably stupid, lazy or greedy, then you need to decide whether the question involves a possible breach by directors of the duty of care or a possible breach by the directors of the duty or loyalty.

Let's consider duty of care first.

4. What Facts Trigger Directors' Duty of Care Issues?

In essence, a board of directors makes decisions and supervises the decisions of others. If an exam fact pattern raises the possibility that:

- the board made a dumb decision,
- the board made a decision without appropriate study and preparation, or
- the board did not spend enough time and effort in supervising others,

then apply the discussion of directors duty of care from parts 5 to 9 below.

5. What Does the Delaware General Corporation Law and the Articles of Incorporation of a Delaware Corporation Say About the Duty of Care?

The Delaware General Corporation Law does not the use the phrase "duty of care" and nowhere establishes a standard of care for directors. Under Delaware law, a director's duty of care is based on case law, not statutory law.

While the Delaware General Corporation Law does not create a director's duty of care, the Delaware statute does provide for the possible elimination of a director's duty of care in the corporation's certificate of incorporation. Under section 102(b)(7), a corporation's certificate of incorporation can provide that directors have no personal liability for breach of duty of care. Such a provision is almost certain to be included in the certificate of incorporation of corporations in the real world, and always possible to be included in the unreal world of law school exam questions.

Delaware also protects directors from liability for breach of duty of care in section 141(e). Under section 141(e) of the Delaware General Corporation Law, directors can escape liability for breach of duty of care if their actions or inactions were based on reasonable reliance on the information and advice of officers, employees, or outside experts. In the event that you have a law school exam question involving (1) a Delaware corporation, (2) without a section 102(b)(7) provision in its certificate of incorporation, and (3) with facts that suggest the board made a decision that resulted in a financial loss to the corporation then look for facts about reliance on officers or outside experts.

6. What Does the MBCA and Articles of Incorporation of an MBCA State Corporation Say About the Duty of Care?

Like section 141(e) of the Delaware General Corporation Law, MBCA section 8.31(e) protects directors from possible duty of care liability if their actions or inactions were based on reasonable reliance on the information and advice of officers, employees, or outside experts. And, like section 102(b)(7) of the Delaware General Corporation Law, MBCA section 2.02(b)(4) permits a corporation in its articles of incorporation to eliminate the personal liability of a director for breach of duty of care.

Unlike the Delaware General Corporation Law, the MBCA does expressly set a standard of care for directors. MBCA section 8.30 requires that in discharging their decision-making function and in discharging their oversight function, directors must "discharge their duties with the care that a person in like position would reasonably believe appropriate under similar circumstances." This seems similar to the duty of care commonly imposed under tort law.

Most of the duty of care cases in BA/BO casebooks involve Delaware corporations and so, under the internal affairs doctrine, apply Delaware law. The next three parts then, 7-9, cover these Delaware law cases.

7. What Is the Business Judgment Rule and How Should the Business Judgment Rule Be Used in Answering Exam Questions About the Merits of a Board of Directors' Decision?

The phrase "business judgment rule" does not appear in either the Delaware General Corporation Statute or the MBCA. Instead, the business judgment rule is a court-created concept. More important, "business judgment rule" is a term that appears in cases involving allegations of breach of duty care by both directors of Delaware corporations and directors of corporations incorporated in a state with the MBCA.

And, most important, the business judgment rule must appear in any exam answer involving litigation over the substantive merits of a board decision. The business judgment rule means that a plaintiff alleging that directors breached their duty of care cannot prevail *solely* by attacking the substantive merits of a board decision. Because of the business judgment rule, a court will not rule as to whether a board decision was a smart decision or a stupid decision when there is no proof that the members of the board have in some way acted badly.

In *Shlensky v. Wrigley*, a shareholder of the Delaware corporation that owned the Chicago Cubs unsuccessfully challenged the board of directors' decision to play all Chicago Cubs' home games in the afternoon. In dismissing the complaint, the court stated:

> "We do not mean to say that we have decided that the decision of the directors was a correct one. That is beyond our jurisdiction and ability. We are merely saying that the decision is one properly before directors and the motives alleged in the amended complaint showed no fraud, illegality or conflict of interest in their making of that decision."

As this statement from *Shlensky* illustrates, "the business judgment rule is not a rule that states boards of directors always make smart decisions, or even provides a presumption that boards of directors have made smart decisions. Rather, the business judgment rule is a rule that limits the role of courts in reviewing the substance of a board of director decision. It is a statement of what courts will not do—a doctrine of abstention."[1] To restate, under the business judgment rule a court will not review the merits of board action when there is no proof that the members of the board have acted badly, i.e., "fraud, illegality or conflict of interest."

There are some cases appearing in some business associations/ organizations casebooks that could be viewed as establishing a "no-win exception" to the "business judgment rule." *Litwin v. Allen* and *Joy v. North* are two such cases.

In *Litwin*, the board of directors of a New York corporation approved the corporation's purchase of securities in another corporation that gave the seller the option to repurchase the securities at the same sales price within six months. Under this deal, the buying corporation would bear the loss if the securities it purchased dropped in value but would not realize any benefit from an increase in value because the seller could (and surely would) buy the securities back at the original sale price.

In *Joy v. North*, the "no-win decision" not protected by the business judgment rule was the decision by the board of directors of a financial institution incorporated in New York to continue providing funding for a commercial real estate customer long after it was clear that the financial institution commercial real estate customer's building project would fail.

There are also some Delaware cases and commentaries that seem to be saying something different about the business judgment rule—that the business judgment rule changes the standard of care for directors' decision-making from ordinary negligence to gross negligence:

- "While the Delaware cases use a variety of terms to describe the applicable standard of care, our

---

[1] Stephen M. Bainbridge, *The Business Judgment Rule as an Abstention Doctrine*, 57 Vand. L. Rev. 83 (2004).

analysis satisfies us that under the business judgment rule director liability is predicated upon concepts of gross negligence."[2]

- "[T]he business judgment rule protects fiduciaries from judicial second-guessing of nearly any ordinary business decision, short of gross negligence or apparent conflict of interest."[3]

These cases and commentaries seem to combine two different problems: problem(1), directors' duty of care liability for decisions that are substantively bad, with problem (2), directors' duty of care liability for decisions that are negligently made.

Shlensky v. Wrigley, discussed above, is an example of problem (1)—not playing baseball games at night which was litigated as a substantively bad decision. *Smith v. Van Gorkom*, discussed below, is an example of problem (2)—approving a sale of the business in a single, short meeting which was litigated as a flawed decision-making process.

8. Can the Board of Directors Breach Its Duty of Care by Carelessly Making a Decision?

Smith v. Van Gorkom is the case most commonly used to illustrate the proposition that a board of directors breaches its duty of care by carelessly making a decision. In that case, the plaintiffs alleged that the Trans Union board of directors' decision to approve and recommend for approval by shareholder a merger transaction in which Trans Union's shareholders received $55 cash per share was a breach of the board's duty of care.

---

2 *Aronson v. Lewis*, 473 A.2d at 812 (Del. 1984).

3 John C. Coates IV, *"Fair Value" as an Avoidable Rule of Corporate Law: Minority Discounts in Conflict Transactions*, 147 U. Pa. L. Rev. 1251, 1316 (1999).

The plaintiffs focused on the directors' decision-making process rather than the merits of the directors' decision. The merger had been negotiated by Van Gorkom, Trans Union's CEO (and director), without the knowledge of the rest of the Trans Union board. The other board members did not know about the merger before the board of directors meeting. A meeting which lasted less than two hours. A meeting at which, in the language of the court, "the Board approved the cash-out merger based solely on Van Gorkom's twenty-minute oral presentation about the merger proposal, and the Board failed to review any documents (or ask for a written summary of the merger terms) before approving." A meeting at which directors neither received nor asked for any written documentation of the basis for the $55 per share price.

The trial court ruled for the defendant directors, finding that the directors' approval of the cash merger fell within the protection of the business judgment rule. The Delaware Supreme Court overruled the trial court and ruled for the plaintiffs, reasoning:

- the business judgment rule protects only "informed decisions";
- gross negligence is the proper standard for determining whether a board decision is an "informed decision";
- the decision-making process of the Trans Union board was grossly negligent.

At the time of the Delaware Supreme Court decision, the basic lesson of the *Van Gorkom* case was that directors of a Delaware corporation face liability for breach of a duty of care if they are grossly negligent in failing to adequately inform themselves.

Shortly after the *Smith v. Van Gorkom* decision, the Delaware legislature added section 102(b)(7) to the Delaware General Corporation statute permitting a Delaware corporation to include a provision in its certificate of incorporation that eliminates the duty of care. The MBCA then authorized similar exculpatory provisions in the articles.

Accordingly, the present practical significance of *Smith v. Van Gorkom* is limited. Today, the basic lesson of *Van Gorkom* is that directors of a Delaware corporation face liability for breach of their duty of care if they are grossly negligent in failing to adequately inform themselves regarding a decision before them, unless that Delaware corporation's certificate of incorporation has eliminated liability for breach of duty of case as permitted by section 102(b)(7).

Note the qualifying phrase "a Delaware corporation." If your exam question involves (i) a sloppy decision making process by the board of (ii) corporation incorporated in an MBCA state (iii) whose articles do not eliminate the duty of care, then you should discuss not only *Smith v. Van Gorkom*, but also MBCA section 8.31(a)(2)(ii)(B). This section provides for liability if "the party asserting liability in a proceeding establishes that:

> (2) the challenged conduct was the result of . . .
>
> > (ii) a decision . . .
> >
> > > (B) as to which the director was not informed to an extent the director reasonably believed appropriate in the circumstance."

If your professor covered MBCA section 8.31(a)(2)(ii)(B), I hope your professor provided an explanation of what "to an extent the director reasonably believed appropriate" means. Courts have yet to provide such an explanation.

To review, when dealing with a fact pattern involving a challenge to a board of directors' decision, look first for an exculpatory provision in the articles/certificate. If there is no such exculpatory provision then determine whether plaintiffs are basing their breach of duty of care argument on (i) the substance of the decision or (ii) the process by which the decision was made.

Understandably, courts will invoke the business judgment rule to avoid reviewing the merits of the BBC board of directors' decisions such as a decision that BBC should sell sausage and mash as well as barbecue. Judges have experience in making decisions about what the law is, not experience in making decisions about whether a restaurant should sell sausage and mash.

However, since courts of law make decisions, judges have experience, if not expertise, in the decision making process. Accordingly, judges will not invoke the business judgment rule to avoid reviewing challenges to the process by which the BBC board of directors made the decision to sell sausage and mash.

The Delaware Chancery Court put it more eloquently in *In re Caremark International Inc. Derivative Litigation* (a case that was probably included in your syllabus):

> "Compliance with a director's duty of care can never appropriately be judicially determined by reference to *the content of the board decision* that leads to a corporate loss, apart from consideration of the . . . rationality of the process employed. That is, whether a judge or jury considering the matter after the fact, believes a decision substantively wrong, or degrees of wrong extending through "stupid" to "egregious" or "irrational", provides no ground for director liability. . . . Thus, the business judgment rule is process oriented and informed by a deep respect for all *good faith* board decisions."

9. Can a Board of Directors Breach Its Duty of Care by Failing to Supervise the Corporation's Compliance with Laws and Regulations and Other Actions of the Corporation's Officers and Employees?

Recall that the board of directors has not only decision-making responsibilities but also oversight responsibilities. Look for a nonfeasance fact pattern—a story suggesting either (i) "no effort to keep advised of the actual conduct of the corporate affairs"[4] or (ii) "failure to implement and monitor information systems or control."[5]

Most business associations/organizations casebooks include *Barnes v. Andrews*, a New York case, as the example of a director who breached his duty of care by neglecting his oversight responsibilities. In that case, Andrews became a director of a corporation that had been formed to manufacture engine starters for Ford motors and aircraft. The company had a facility, had personnel in place, "hired at substantial salaries," but during the time that Andrews served as a director, the company made no engine starters and Andrews made no efforts to find out why the company was not making any engine starters. When the company was unable to pay its creditors, a receiver was appointed.

Barnes, the receiver, sued Andrews to recover money to pay the corporation's creditors, alleging Andrews' breach of the duty of care. Judge Learned Hand found that Andrews breached his duty of care to the corporation but nonetheless held that Andrews was not liable to the corporation.

There are two main points to *Barnes v. Andrews*. First, a director's duty of care includes a duty "in general to keep advised

---

[4] *Barnes v. Andrews*, 298 F. 614, 616 (SDNY 1924).

[5] *In re Caremark International, Inc. Derivative Litigation*, 698 A.2d 959 (Del Ch. 1996).

of the conduct of corporate affairs." The court holds that Andrews breached it. Basically, Andrews was, at best, lazy in his performance as a director.

Second, and more importantly, Andrews is not liable. The burden is on the plaintiff to show not only that Andrews breached the duty of care, but also that Andrews's breach of duty caused a loss to the corporation. The plaintiff must show that "the performance of the defendant's duties would have avoided loss, and what loss it would have avoided."

It is understandable that the plaintiff in *Barnes v. Andrews*, failed to make such a showing. Judge Hand's standard in *Barnes v. Andrews* is similar to the "but for" cause-in-fact standard you learned in tort, but it is generally much easier to prove the cause of an accident than it is to prove the cause of a corporation's loss. It is understandable that in *Barnes v. Andrews*, Judge Hand suggests that there is no lack of oversight case in which the plaintiff has met this burden of proof.

The MBCA is consistent with *Barnes*. A director is not liable for lack of oversight unless the plaintiff bears the burden of showing both the lack of oversight and the causal connection, i.e., that damages to the corporation were "proximately caused by the director's challenged conduct," MBCA section 8.31(b)(1).

The Delaware cases on directors' oversight failures that are covered in a basic business association/organizations class are different. These Delaware cases involve (i) large corporations and allegations that (ii) the board (not any one particular director) has failed to (iii) implement or maintain systems to monitor operations. Delaware cases regularly refer to the board's oversight duties as "*Caremark* duties."

You only need to read the remainder of part 9 if your prof assigned the *Caremark* case.

Caremark International, Inc. was in the health care business. A substantial part of the revenues generated by Caremark's businesses was derived from Medicare and Medicaid reimbursement programs. Caremark paid $250,000,000 in fines for its employees' violations of Medicare and Medicaid rules. A lawsuit was filed alleging that the Caremark board of directors should be held liable to the corporation for the $250,000,000 because of the board of directors' oversight failures. The case was settled.

In upholding the settlement in which the members of the board of directors of Caremark paid zero dollars to the corporation, the Delaware Supreme Court made the following statement about director's oversight duties: "a director's obligation includes a duty to attempt in good faith to assure that a corporate information and reporting system, which the board concludes is adequate, exists, and that failure to do so under some circumstances may, in theory at least, render a director liable for losses caused by non-compliance with applicable legal standards."

Did you catch the three "weasel words" in the above statement? First, the court used the permissive "may," instead of the mandatory "will." Second, the court inserted the qualifying phrase "in theory." Third, the court added yet another qualifying phrase, "under some circumstances." What are "some circumstances?"

Stone v. Ritter, a later Delaware Supreme Court case involving allegations of board of directors' liability for oversight failure, expressly affirms *Caremark* and explains "some circumstances" with the following statement: "*Caremark* articulates the necessary conditions predicate for director oversight liability: (a) the directors utterly failed to implement any reporting or information system or controls; or (b) having implemented such a system or controls, consciously failed to monitor or oversee its operations thus disabling themselves from being informed of risks or problems requiring their attention. In either case, imposition of liability *requires a showing that the directors knew that they were not discharging their fiduciary obligations*. When directors fail to act in the face of a known duty to act demonstrating a conscious disregard for their responsibilities they breach their duty of loyalty by failing to discharge that fiduciary obligation in good faith," (emphasis added).

Please reread this excerpt.

First, notice that the plaintiff has the burden of proving not only that the monitoring system or actual monitoring was inadequate but also that the directors knew that the monitoring was inadequate, i.e., "conscious disregard." How can the plaintiff prove that the defendant directors knew that they were doing something wrong? That is why the Delaware Supreme Court in *Stone* granted the defendants' motion to dismiss. That is why the Delaware Supreme Court in *Caremark* stated "the theory here advanced (liability for breach of duty of oversight) is possibly the most difficult theory in corporation law upon which a plaintiff might hope to win a judgment."

Second, notice that in *Stone v. Ritter*, the Delaware Supreme Court interpreted the *Caremark* duty of oversight (which the *Caremark* case based on a duty of care) as a duty of loyalty. That is exam-important.

Recall that Delaware General Corporation Statute section 107(b)(7) permits a Delaware corporation to eliminate the directors' liability for breach of a duty of care by so providing in the corporation's certificate of incorporation. Section 102(b)(7) goes on to state that "such provision shall not eliminate or limit the liability of a director . . . for breach of the director's duty of loyalty." Thus, in an exam fact pattern involving lack of oversight by the directors of a Delaware corporation that has an exculpatory provision in its certificate, that exculpatory provision will be irrelevant under *Stone v. Ritter*.

10. What Facts Suggest That a Director Has Breached Her Duty of Loyalty to the Corporation?

Look for a fact pattern in which a director uses her position as a director to gain some individual monetary gain or other personal advantage. More specifically, watch for either (1) the director's usurping a "corporate opportunity" [e.g., BBC, a corporation, owns and operates a restaurant that needs to expand. S, the owner of land adjacent to the restaurant, contacts D because D is a director of BBC and offers to sell BBC the land that is adjacent to BBC's restaurant. D buys the land for D's own real estate development company, D Realty Inc., without ever mentioning the opportunity to BBC's other directors] or (2) the corporation's entering into an "interested director transaction" [e.g., BBC corporation buys land from D Realty, Inc., a corporation owned by one of its directors at an above market price] or (3) (much less likely because it is too easy) a director's competing with the corporation [e.g., D, a director of the BBC corporation, opens D's own restaurant in the same neighborhood as BBC's restaurant].

11. Can a Delaware Corporation's Certificate of Incorporation or an MBCA Act State Corporation's Article of Incorporation Eliminate a Director's Liability for (1) Usurping a Corporate Opportunity, (2) Entering into an Interested Director Transaction, or (3) Competing with the Corporation?

The Delaware General Corporation Statute and the MBCA use different words to state the same general rule: a corporation cannot in its certificate or articles eliminate a director's liability for (1) usurping a corporate opportunity, (2) entering into an interested director transaction, or (3) competing with the corporation.

12. What Does Delaware Corporate Law on Usurping a "Corporate Opportunity" Add to *Meinhard v. Salmon*?

Recall *Meinhard v. Salmon*? Of course not.

There, two men were in a business venture together. They had leased, improved, and were operating a building. Meinhard was an investor only, whereas Salmon was also the managing coadventurer. Gerry, the owner of the building, approached Salmon about leasing, improving, and operating adjacent properties. Salmon took the opportunity for himself, without even telling Meinhard about it. When Meinhard learned of this, he demanded to be included in the new deal and sued Salmon for breach of the duty of loyalty. Meinhard prevailed.

In finding a breach of duty of loyalty in *Meinhard*, the court (Judge Cardozo) emphasized three facts:

(1) the similarity between the new opportunity and what the business was already doing;

(2) the opportunity came to Meinhard because of the business he was in with Salmon;

(3) Salmon was the managing coadventurer.

Even though the business in *Meinhard v. Salmon* was not a corporation and Judge Cardozo never uses the term "corporate opportunity," *Meinhard v. Salmon* is commonly mentioned in corporate opportunity cases and should be mentioned in any exam answer you write about usurping a corporate opportunity.

And, if the corporation in your exam fact pattern is a Delaware corporation, then you should also mention *Guth v. Loft, Inc.*. Guth is the leading Delaware case on usurping a corporate opportunity.

Guth was the President and a director of Loft Inc., a corporation that manufactured and sold candies, syrups, food and beverages, including Coca-Cola (but not Pepsi-Cola). Guth took for himself the opportunity to purchase the Pepsi-Cola formula and trademark. In finding that Guth violated the "rule of corporate opportunity," the Delaware Supreme Court stated:

> "[I]f there is presented to a corporate officer or director a business opportunity *which the corporation* is financially able *to undertake*, is, from its nature, in the line of the corporation's business and is of practical advantage to it, is one in which the corporation has an interest or a reasonable expectancy, and, by embracing the opportunity, the self-interest of the officer or director will be brought into conflict with that of his corporation, the law will not permit him to seize the opportunity." (emphasis added)

Note the underscored language. There is no comparable language about Meinhard's financial ability or lack thereof[6] in *Meinhard v. Salmon*.

More important, there is no comparable language in the American Law Institute's Principles of Corporate Governance.

[6] Apparently there were no issues about Meinhard's financial ability.

13. What Does the American Law Institute's Principles of Corporate Governance Provisions on Corporate Opportunity Add to *Meinhard v. Salmon*?

The American Law Institute's ("ALI") Principles of Corporate Governance, like the ALI's Restatements, are binding only to the extent adopted by courts. In *Northeast Harbor Golf Club, Inc. v. Harris,* a case included in most BA/BO casebooks, the Maine Supreme Court rejected *Guth v. Loft, Inc.* and applied the ALI's Principles of Corporate Governance instead.

Harris was president of a Maine corporation which operated a golf club. She purchased two parcels of land near the club, the Gilpin property and the Smallidge property. Harris was approached about buying the Gilpin property because she was president of the corporation and the seller thought the corporation would be interested in the purchase to maintain a buffer around the club and for development. Possible sale of the Smallidge property came to Harris's attention when a person she played golf with told her about it.

The trial court relied on *Guth v. Loft, Inc.*, the Delaware case discussed above, and held that Harris had not usurped a corporate opportunity because (1) the land was not in the corporation's "line of business" and (2) the corporation lacked the financial wherewithal to purchase the property. On appeal, the Supreme Court of Maine reversed and remanded, rejecting the *Guth* approach and adopting the ALI Principles of Corporate Governance instead.

The ALI Principles of Corporate Governance differs significantly from *Guth* and later Delaware cases following Guth. Delaware cases use a balancing of factors to determine (1) what is a "corporate opportunity" and (2) what a director or officer must do before she can take that opportunity for herself. On the other hand, The ALI

Principles of Corporate Governance has specific rules as to (1) what is a corporate opportunity and (2) what a director or officer must do before she can take that opportunity for herself.

The four such ALI rules that were most important in *Northeast Harbor Golf Club, Inc. v. Harris,* (and most likely to be important on your exam) are:

(1) a business prospect is a "corporate opportunity" if the director or corporate officer learns of the opportunity because she is a director or officer—even if the opportunity is not in the corporation's line of business, and

(2) similarly, a business prospect is a "corporate opportunity" if it is closely related to a business in which the corporation is now engaged or expects to engage, regardless of how the director or officer learns of the opportunity, and

(3) a director or corporate officer must always offer a "corporate opportunity" to the corporation and the corporation must reject it before taking it for herself, and

(4) whether the corporation is financially able to pursue the business prospect is irrelevant to the questions of whether a business prospect is a "corporate opportunity" or whether the director or corporate officer must offer the "corporate opportunity" to the corporation.

To review, apply the ALI principles and then the Delaware law to the following two hypotheticals:

(1) D, a director of the BBC corporation which owns and operates a restaurant learns from the coach of her daughter's soccer team (who does not know that D

is a director of BBC) of an opportunity to buy the land adjacent to BBC's restaurant.

(2) D, a director of the BBC corporation which owns and operates a restaurant learns of an opportunity to invest in minor league soccer team. He learns of this opportunity because he is a director of the BBC corporation.

Under the ALI principles, the business prospect in both (1) and (2) are corporate opportunities which must be offered to BBC and turned down by BBC before D can take the opportunities.

Under Delaware case law, whether the business prospects in (1) and (2) are corporate opportunities and whether D must disclose these opportunities to BBC is a factual question to be decided by reasonable inference from objective facts, including the financial ability of BBC to pursue these business prospects.

14. What Are "Interested Director Transactions" and How Do the MBCA and the Delaware General Corporation Statute Deal with "Interested Director Transactions"?

An "interested director transaction" is a transaction between a corporation and one or more of its directors (or officers or controlling shareholders), or between the corporation and an entity in which one or more of its directors has a material financial interest. For example, D owns Redacre. D sells Redacre to BBC, a corporation. D is a member of the board of directors of BBC corporation. D's sale of Redacre to BBC would be an "interested director transaction." Or, to use the language of the MBCA, D's sale of Redacre to the corporation for which D is a director would be a "director's conflicting interest transaction."

While the language of the relevant MBCA provisions—sections 8.60 to 8.63—is different from the language of the relevant Delaware provision—section 144, the basic approach of the two statutes is similar in at least three respects:

(1) Even if a corporation enters into a transaction with one of its directors that transaction will not always be avoided, and that interested director will not always be held liable.

Some interested directors transactions are good for the corporation. For example, a director might be willing to sell to the corporation at a discount or make a loan to a corporation even though the corporation's credit rating makes it impossible to obtain a loan from a financial institution.

(2) If a transaction is an interested director transaction, the director escapes judicial relief against her or the transaction by proving "the entire fairness" of the transaction to the corporation at the time of the transaction.

Notice that the defendant has the burden of proving fairness at the time of transaction. More important, note the term "entire fairness." The words "entire fairness" do not appear in the Delaware General Corporation Statute but do appear in the cases applying Delaware law and should appear in any exam answer you write.

And, begin that answer by noting that under the entire fairness standard, the defendant directors have the burden of proving both (1) procedural fairness, i.e., that the agreement process was fair (sometimes referred to as "fair dealing") and (2) substantive fairness, i.e., that the price was fair. While your answer should treat "fair dealing" and "fair price" as separate components, a court's concern about the deal process often affects its conclusion about the fairness of the deal's substance.

HMG/Courtland Properties, Inc. v. Gray, a Delaware case which appears in business associations/organizations casebooks, provides an easy to understand illustration. There, HMG sold property to a company owned by two of its directors, Gray and Fieber, and others. Not only did director Gray not disclose to the HMG board that he owned an interest in the company that was buying property from HMG, Gray himself negotiated the deal on behalf of HMG.

Even though it was obvious that the deal process was flawed the court also discussed the fairness of the price:

> "the defendants misconceive their burden. On the record before me, I obviously cannot conclude that HMG received a shockingly low price in the Transactions or that the prices paid were not within the low end of the range of possible prices that might have been paid in negotiated arms-length deals. In that narrow sense, the defendants have proven that the price was "fair." But that proof does not necessarily satisfy their burden under the entire fairness standard. The defendants have failed to persuade me that HMG would not have gotten a materially higher value for Wallingford and the Grossman's Portfolio had Gray and Fieber come clean about Gray's interest. That is, they have not convinced me that their misconduct did not taint the price to HMG's disadvantage."

In other words, "fair price" requires more than proof that the price was reasonable. Instead, the entire fairness defense to a suit challenging an interested director transaction requires that the defendant prove that the price would not have been better if the deal process had not been flawed.

Many casebooks also include *Weinberger v. UOP, Inc.*, a less obvious example of an "interested director" transaction—a merger of a partially owned subsidiary into a parent. There, Signal owned 50.5% of the outstanding stock of UOP and wanted to acquire the other 49.5% in a cash out merger.

Signal, as majority shareholder of UOP, controlled the election of all of the UOP directors. Two of the Signal directors were also UOP directors. More important, those two directors prepared a report for Signal using UOP data that showed that $24 a share would be a fair price for Signal to pay for the rest of the UOP stock and did not provide this report to the UOP board.

Not surprisingly, when the Signal board offered a merger price of $21 a share (i.e., UOP would merge into Signal, UOP would thus cease to exist, and the shareholders of UOP would receive $21 a share), the UOP board accepted the offer. Not surprisingly, Weinberger brought a class action on behalf of all of the minority shareholders of UOP claiming breach of a fiduciary duty.

The Delaware Supreme Court held for the plaintiffs applying the entire fairness standard and stating:

> "where directors of a Delaware corporation are on both sides of a transaction, they are required to demonstrate their utmost good faith and the most scrupulous inherent fairness of the bargain. . . . The concept of fairness has two basic aspects: fair dealing and fair price. . . . However, the test for fairness is not a bifurcated one as between fair dealing and price. All aspects of the issue must be examined as a whole since the question is one of entire fairness."

Think about the costs of litigating the "entire fairness" of a complicated transaction such as the merger of UOP into Signal. The transaction occurred early in 1978. The lawsuit was filed shortly thereafter. The trial concluded late in 1980. Extensive and expensive expert testimony on disputed issues of valuation of UOP as of the time of the merger were needed.

(3) Alternatively, if a transaction is an interested director transaction, the director escapes judicial relief against her or the transaction if the transaction is approved by a majority of the disinterested directors or by an independent board committee with at least two disinterested directors or by the disinterested holders of a majority of shares after full disclosure.

Under both the Delaware General Corporation Statute and the MBCA, an interested director transaction will not be subject to an entire fairness standard if the transaction was approved by a majority of the disinterested directors or the disinterested holders of a majority of the shares after full disclosure. Director approval or shareholder approval will have this "cleansing" effect only if there has been full disclosure of the conflicting interest.

To illustrate, Larry owns Readacre and is one of the four directors of BBC. Larry sells Redacre to BBC. If, after disclosure of Larry's ownership of Redacre, two of the other three BBC directors authorize the transaction, then D does not have to prove the "entire fairness" of the transaction. Similarly, if Larry owns Redacre and owns 100 shares of BBC stock and Moe, Curly and Shemp own the other 1200 outstanding share. Larry sells Redacre to BB. Larry does not have to prove "entire fairness" if a majority of the shares owned by shareholders other than Larry approve the transaction after disclosure.

There are some relatively minor differences between the Delaware General Corporation Statute provisions and the MBCA provisions on approval of interested director transactions by directors or shareholders. The MBCA uses the terms "qualified directors" and "qualified shareholders" instead of "disinterested director" and "disinterested shareholders." Also, the MBCA provisions on what is required to establish a quorum and what constitutes a majority are less ambiguous than the Delaware provisions—this is the kind of detail that only a putz would test.[7]

To review, when a director of the corporation has a personal interest in a transaction with the corporation, that transaction must be approved by disinterested people. The disinterested people can be either (i) other members of the board of directors who are disinterested, (ii) other shareholders who are disinterested, or (iii) a judge. If (i) or (ii), then there must be disclosure. If (iii), then there is the "entire fairness" standard review by a judge.

15. What Is Not Obvious About the Legal Consequences of a Director's Competing with Her Corporation?

Nothing. Obviously, a director cannot compete with a corporation while she is a director of that corporation. A director's competing with the corporation she serves is a breach of the duty of loyalty.

If BBC is in the barbecue business and Moe is a director of BBC, Moe, also a fiduciary of BBC, obviously cannot own or open a competing barbecue business while he is a BBC director. What Moe does after he is no longer a BBC director will be governed by the contract law covering covenants not to compete, and the tort law regarding trade secrets.

---

[7] Just in case, your business associations/organizations prof is Professor Putz, under the Delaware General Corporation Statute it is not clear whether the quorum is made up of a majority of the disinterested or a majority of all. And, under the Delaware General Corporation Statute, it is not clear whether the majority vote is a majority of all disinterested or a majority of all disinterested that vote.

16. What Does "Good Faith" Add to a Director's Duty of Care and Duty of Loyalty?

There is no question that a director must act in good faith. The term "good faith" appears throughout the Delaware General Corporation Statute and the MBCA.

There are, however, unanswered questions about the precise scope of the good faith obligation. Neither the Delaware General Corporation Statute nor the MBCA defines "good faith."

There are two Delaware cases with dicta that should be included in an essay question answer discussion of good faith: (1) *In re The Walt Disney Company Derivative Litigation* and (2) *Stone v. Ritter*.

The *Disney* case involved a challenge to the Walt Disney Company's board of directors' approval of $140 million of termination pay to outgoing president Michael Ovitz. Plaintiffs' amended complaint alleged bad faith. The plaintiffs' allegation of bad faith was critical to the court's denying defendants' motion to dismiss.

After section 102(b)(7) was added to the Delaware General Corporation Statute enabling a Delaware corporation to add a provision to its articles eliminating director liability for breach of the duty of care, the Walt Disney Company, like most Delaware corporations, added such an exculpatory provision to its certificate. Section 102(b)(7), however, does not permit a corporation to "eliminate or limit the liability of a director . . . for acts or omissions not in good faith."

The *Disney* case ruled that the complaint pleaded facts supporting a claim for liability based on the directors' not acting in good faith. More specifically, the court indicated that the facts necessary to support a lack of good faith are facts that "suggest that the defendant directors consciously and intentionally disregarded their responsibilities."

Stone v. Ritter, discussed earlier, is important for stating that the duty to act in good faith is a part of the duty of loyalty. This expands—at least in Delaware—the scope of the duty of loyalty.

Traditionally, the duty of loyalty has been limited to situations in which a director realizes a personal financial gain at the expense of the corporation—taking an opportunity from the corporation, profiting from a transaction with the corporation, competing with the corporation. After *Stone v. Ritter*, there is a lack of good faith and thus breach of a duty of loyalty whenever a director *knowingly*, for any reason, does not act in the corporation's best interest, regardless of whether the director realizes a personal financial gain. The important word is "knowingly."

Disney, *Stone v. Ritter*, and other cases on good faith included in business associations/organizations casebooks are Delaware cases. There is not a comparable body of MBCA case law.

This chapter has summarized the legal obligations of directors to corporations. The next chapter on shareholder derivative suits focuses on who enforces those obligations.

CHAPTER 18

What You Need to Know About the Law of Shareholder Derivative Actions

To understand the law of shareholder derivative actions, you need to remember some of the law of corporations you covered in Chapters 16 and 17. Specifically, the law of corporations related to corporate governance:

- a corporation is owned by its shareholders;
- even though a corporation is owned by its shareholders, a corporation is governed by its board of directors—a corporation's decisions are made by its board of directors;
- the business judgment rule generally precludes judicial review of the merits of a decision by the board of directors;
- among the many decisions made by a corporation's board of directors is the decision whether to sue someone;

- the business judgment rule generally precludes judicial review of merits of a decision by a corporation's board of directors not to sue;
- the business judgment rule, however, does not apply to all decisions by a board of directors. The business judgment rule applies only when directors make a decision without a conflict of interest.

To review, consider the following two hypotheticals:

First hypothetical: Alpha, Inc. is a critical supplier of Baker Corporation. Alpha, Inc. breaches a supply contract with Baker Corporation by making a late delivery. The contract included "time is of the essence" and "liquidated damages" provisions.

The Baker Corporation's board of directors decide against suing Alpha, Inc., believing that maintaining a strong relationship with a critical supplier was more important than recovering liquidated damages. The business judgment rule would apply to that decision.

Second hypothetical: The members of the Baker board of directors open their own business that competes directly with the Bake Corporation. Not surprisingly, the members of the Baker Corporation board of directors do not decide to sue themselves. Obviously, the decision by the Baker Corporation board not to sue themselves for breaching their duty of loyalty to the Baker Corporation by competing with the Baker Corporation would not be protected by the business judgment rule.

What is less obvious about the second hypothetical is who can sue the directors of Baker Corporation for breaching the duty of loyalty that they owe to the Baker Corporation. The answer to who can sue the Baker board of directors in the second hypothetical is the Baker shareholders by bringing a shareholder derivative action.

In theory, a Baker shareholder could also bring a shareholder derivative action against Delta Corporation in the first hypothetical.

In the real world, nearly every shareholder derivative action claim involves allegations of wrongdoings by the members of the board of directors themselves.

You need to know four things about a shareholder derivative action:

(1) Whether a suit initiated by a shareholder should be treated as a shareholder derivative suit

(2) Who "wins" in a shareholder derivative action

(3) What the special procedural requirements for a shareholder derivative action are

(4) What the role of a special litigation committee is

1. What Factors Determine Whether a Lawsuit Initiated by Shareholders Should Be Treated as a Shareholder Derivative Action or a Direct Action?

When a shareholder initiates a derivative suit, they are suing to vindicate a corporation's legal rights. Their status as a plaintiff derives from the corporation's legal right to be a plaintiff and their ownership interest in the corporation.

At other times, a shareholder sues to vindicate their own legal rights. Such a lawsuit is commonly referred to as a direct lawsuit. In determining whether a pending action is a derivative suit or a direct suit, courts generally ask two closely related questions: (1) who sustained a direct harm and (2) who should receive relief.

And, in determining whether a pending suit is a derivative suit or a direct suit, the number of shareholders initiating the action is irrelevant. If thousands of shareholders suffered the same direct harm, they can bring a class action, which is a form of direct suit.

Sometimes, it can be hard to determine whether a claim is direct or derivative. The example of such a hard case used in most casebooks is *Eisenberg v. Flying Tiger Line, Inc.*, an action by a stockholder on behalf of himself and all other stockholders to enjoin consummation of a complicated merger transaction. If your prof did not assign the *Eisenberg* case (and she should not have), then you do not have to read the next four paragraphs.

(1) In *Eisenberg*, before the challenged transaction, the plaintiff was the shareholder of a corporation that owned and operated an airline. After the merger, the plaintiff would hold stock in a holding company that owned a corporation that owned and operated an airline.

(2) After the merger, as a minority shareholder of a holding company, that owned a corporation that owned and operated an airline, plaintiff would not be able to influence the operation of the airline. Prior to the merger, plaintiff, as a shareholder of the corporation that owned an airline, has some say in the operation of the airline—e.g., election of its directors, vote on amendments to its certificate of incorporation. After the challenged transaction, the plaintiff would instead own stock in a corporation that owned and operated an airline—a holding company, not an operating company. Instead of voting for the women and men (probably just men) who would be running an airline, he would be voting for the women and men who would be running a holding company and they would vote for the women and men who would be running the airline.

(3) The defendant alleged that the plaintiff's cause of action was derivative. The trial court agreed with the defendant's characterization and dismissed the case because the plaintiff had failed to post security for the corporation's expenses—a New York procedural requirement for shareholder derivative suits.

(4) Note that the focus of the plaintiff's complaint was on the impact of the merger on the shareholder and rights of the shareholder, not the impact of the merger on the corporation. That is what the Second Circuit noted in reversing the trial court and holding that the lawsuit was a direct action and not a derivative action. The Second Circuit said:

> "where a shareholder sues on behalf of himself and all others similarly situated to * * * enjoin a proposed merger or consolidation * * * he is not enforcing a derivative right; he is, by an appropriate type of class suit enforcing a right common to all the shareholders which runs against the corporation. . . . [Plaintiff's] position is even stronger than it would be in the ordinary merger case. In routine merger circumstances the stockholders retain a voice in the operation of the company, albeit a corporation other than their original choice. Here, however, the reorganization deprived him and other minority stockholders of any voice in the affairs of their previously existing operating company."

Suits by shareholders alleging denial of voting rights or nonpayment of declared dividends are easier and more frequently tested examples of direct suits. Denial of shareholders' voting rights or nonpayment of declared dividends does not harm the corporation. The shareholder and only the shareholder was harmed, and the harm is direct. Any judgment—either damages or some other remedy—should be for the shareholders.

By contrast, suits alleging directors' breach of duty of care or duty of loyalty are easy examples of derivative suits. Directors owe fiduciary duties to the corporation.

When, for example, the members of the Baker Corporation board of directors open their own business that competes directly with Baker Corporation, the corporation is the one that has been directly harmed because the directors' competing business has caused the Baker Corporation to have less money that it should. Any harm to the shareholders is derivative of the harm to the corporation. The shareholders are indirectly harmed because their interest in the company has a somewhat lower value than it would have if the directors had not breached their fiduciary duty by competing with the corporation. Any judgment—either damages or some other remedy—should be for the corporation.

One more time—suits alleging directors' breach of duty of care or duty of loyalty are derivative suits. Indeed nearly every shareholder derivative suit involves allegations of wrongdoings by directors.

2. Who Wins in a Shareholder Derivative Action?

The corporation is supposed to be the winner in a successful shareholder derivative action. As stated above, in a derivative action, the plaintiff shareholder(s) is asserting the corporation's claim and so if the plaintiff shareholder(s) prevails in a shareholder derivative action, any damages should be paid to the corporation and not the plaintiff shareholder(s).

What then would motivate a shareholder of a corporation—especially a shareholder of a corporation with thousands, if not millions of outstanding shares, to go through all of the work of preparing and presenting a case and get nothing for themselves? The possibility that the book value of their stock increases minimally? Altruism? It is a hard question to come up with a realistic answer.

The more important, and easier to answer, question is what motivates an attorney to recruit a shareholder to serve as plaintiff in a shareholder derivative suit. Attorneys' fees is of course the answer.

And, in the "real world," it is not uncommon for the attorney for the plaintiff to be the real winner in a shareholder derivative action. The court can order the corporation to pay the fees of the attorney for the plaintiff if the case resulted in a substantial benefit to the corporation.

Your class may have considered the *Caremark* case. There the attorney for the plaintiffs brought a shareholder derivative action seeking the recovery of $250,000,000 from the Caremark board of directors, alleging that the corporation paid $250,000,000 of fines because of the board's breach of its oversight duties. The opinion approves a settlement of the suit in which the corporation received no money but instead "very modest benefits"—"a more centralized, active supervisory system in the future." The approved settlement also provided for the corporation's payment of $816,000 to the plaintiffs' attorneys—"normal hourly rates plus a premium of 15% of that amount to reflect the limited degree of real contingency in the undertaking."

3. What Are the Special Procedural Requirements for Commencing and Ending a Shareholder Derivative Lawsuit?

State corporate statutes and rules of civil procedures set out numerous special procedural requirements for commencing and ending a derivative action. Like the rules governing class actions, some of these procedural requirements for shareholder derivative suits reflect a concern about plaintiff lawyers' recruiting a shareholder client to bring a shareholder derivative to generate fees for the lawyers, not to right a wrong to a corporation.

As with class actions, there is a "contemporaneous ownership" requirement for a shareholder derivative action. The plaintiff in a shareholder derivative suit must be a shareholder at the time the shareholder derivative suit was brought and, subject to limited exceptions, must also have owned the stock when the claim arose.

As with class action, the shareholder bringing the derivative action must show that she will adequately represent the interest of the corporation. Similarly, statutes and rules governing shareholder derivative actions, like statutes and rules governing class actions, require that the suit cannot be dismissed or settled without the court's approval.[1]

In addition, there are procedural requirements for commencing a shareholder derivative action that reflect corporate government concerns. Generally, the board of directors makes the decisions for a corporation. Shareholder derivative litigation is, in essence, a change in the corporate governance mechanism.

A shareholder derivative lawsuit takes the power to make a decision for the corporation from the board of directors, where it normally is vested, and gives the power to make the decisions for the corporation regarding this litigation to a single shareholder. Accordingly, the procedural requirement in all states that the shareholder make a demand on the board of directors of the corporation that it bring the suit prior to the shareholder's filing a derivative suit would seem to make sense.

The demand is essentially a letter from the shareholder to the board of directors, explaining the grounds for the corporation's suing and asking the board of directors to bring the suit. At first

---

[1] New York and a few other states have an additional procedural requirement—security for expenses—designed to prevent suits designed to extort settlements favorable to the plaintiff's attorney. In a New York shareholder derivative action, the corporation can demand that the plaintiff shareholder post security to cover the defendant's expenses unless the plaintiff shareholder owns at least 5% of the outstanding stock of any class of the corporation's stock or the stock that the plaintiff owns is worth at least $50,000. The only way that I can imagine this to be relevant to an exam question is that your professor is desperate for true/false questions or multiple choice questions and asks an objective question that requires you to know the procedural requirement invoked by the defendant in *Eisenberg v. Flying Tiger Line, Inc.*

blush, requiring a demand does not seem like a big deal. The shareholder just needs to (i) send the demand letter, (ii) wait for the board of directors to reject the demand, and (iii) then bring the suit herself as a shareholder derivative suit.

Nonetheless, in Delaware shareholders rarely make a demand before filing a shareholder derivative suit. Under Delaware law, a stockholder seeking to bring a derivative action must either make a demand on the board of directors to bring a suit on behalf of the corporation OR, alternatively, show that making a demand on the board would be futile.

The problem with a shareholder's pursuing the demand alternative is that Delaware courts treat the shareholder's making a demand as a concession by the shareholder that the board of directors is free from conflict. Whether to initiate litigation to pursue the claims in a stockholder's demand is then left to the board's business judgment. And, when the board of directors refuses the shareholder's demand that the corporation initiate litigation, a shareholder wishing to pursue the litigation must somehow first rebut the business judgment rule presumptions given to the board's decision.

Delaware shareholders rarely make a demand before filing a shareholder derivative suit. Instead, Delaware shareholders typically file the derivative suit and assert that the making of such a demand would be futile.

Under United Foods v. Zuckerberg which is now in most BA casebooks published after 2022, the demand is excused as futile if any ONE of the three following questions is answered "yes" for at least 1/2 of the members of the board

(1) Did the director personally benefit from the conduct that is the subject of the litigation?

(2) Does the director face a substantial likelihood of liability from the litigation?

(3) Does the director lack independence from someone who either benefitted from the conduct that is the subject of the litigation or faces a substantial likelihood of liability from the litigation?

The MBCA takes a different approach. Subject to a very limited exception[2], the MBCA requires that a pre-suit demand must be made in every shareholder derivative case. The MBCA's approach is also different from Delaware in that, under the MBCA, a board's rejection of plaintiff's demand will not be entitled to the judicial deference of the business judgment rule.

4. What Is the Role of a Special Litigation Committee?

Whether the shareholder derivative suit is filed without first making a demand on the board or after making a demand on the board, the board of directors' usual response to a shareholder derivative suit is to file a motion to dismiss. To bolster its chances of prevailing on the motion to dismiss, the board often forms a special litigation committee (SLC).

Under the Delaware General Corporation Statute and the MBCA, the board of directors can delegate governance over a particular decision to a subcommittee of some of the directors. An SLC is such a subcommittee of independent directors—often new directors brought on to the board specifically to serve on the SLC—that conducts its own, independent review of the complaint to

---

[2] Under the MBCA, a shareholder derivative action can be filed by the shareholder without her first making a demand on the board of directors of the corporation if the delay resulting from making such a demand would cause "irreparable injury" to the corporation. The example of "irreparable injury" used by most business associations/organizations law professors is the statute of limitations on the claim is about to (or, if your professor is a true Southerner, "fixin to") expire.

recommend whether the litigation is in the best interest of the corporation.

A SLC's recommendation that the case be dismissed raises two possible questions for the trial court judge in a shareholder derivative action.

The first question is was the SLC truly independent and acting in good faith. Under both Delaware law and the MBCA, the corporation has the burden of showing the independence and good faith of the SLC.

The second question is what deference should the court give to a truly independent SLC's recommendation that the shareholder derivative action be dismissed. The MBCA expressly answers this second question in MBCA section 7.44 which states that the court "shall dismiss a derivative proceeding on motion of the corporation if [an SLC] . . . determines in good faith after conducting a reasonable inquiry upon which its conclusions are based that the maintenance of the derivative proceeding is not in the best interest of the corporation. . . ." This seems consistent with the business judgment rule—the court deferring to the business judgment of the board (or subcommittee of the board) rather than interjecting its own business judgment.

The Delaware General Corporation Statute, unlike the MBCA, does not expressly answer the second question. And, there is Delaware case law supporting an answer to the second question different from the MBCA's—supporting the judge's independent review of the merits of the SLC's recommendation that the shareholder derivative suit be dismissed.

In *Zapata Corp. v. Maldonado*, the Delaware Supreme Court stated:

> "The Court should apply a two-step test to the motion. First, the Court should inquire into the independence and

> good faith of the committee and the bases supporting its conclusions. . . . The second step, [t]he Court should determine, applying its own independent business judgment, whether the motion should be granted. This means, of course, that instances could arise where a committee can establish its independence and sound bases for its good faith decisions and still have the corporation's motion denied."

Zapata's second step is not only inconsistent with the MBCA but also inconsistent with the business judgment rule. And Delaware courts don't always act consistently with *Zapata*.

Just four years after the *Zapata* decision, the Delaware Supreme Court in *Kaplan v. Wyatt* explained, "Proceeding to the second step of the *Zapata* analysis is wholly within the discretion of the court." Since *Kaplan,* Delaware courts have generally not proceeded to the second step.

In sum, remember you are taking a class in business associations/organizations, not a class in civil procedure. Unless your B.A. teacher is a Civil Procedure teacher "drafted" by a desperate dean to teach B.A.

The law of shareholder derivative suits is a part of your business associations/organizations class because shareholder derivative litigation raises a basic corporate governance question—when should a shareholder, rather than the board of directors, be making a decision for the corporation. The basic question in every shareholder derivative action is who gets to make the decision about whether the corporation should sue. And, the usual answer is that, unless there is something rotten in the boardroom, the board of directors should make the decision.

CHAPTER 19

What You Need to Know About How Insurance, Indemnification, and the Articles of Incorporation Protect a Director from Bearing the Financial Consequences of Breach of Fiduciary Duty

If you understand Chapters 17 and 18, you understand the many substantive and procedural obstacles to a plaintiff's obtaining a judgment against a director of a corporation for breach of a fiduciary duty. And, if you understand this chapter, you will understand the reasons that it is unlikely that any such judgment will be paid by the director themselves.

1. What Is the Law Governing Director and Officer Insurance?

Just as some insurance companies sell automobile liability insurance that covers claims made against you based on what you allegedly have done wrong as a driver, other insurance companies sell director and officer liability insurance (D & O insurance) that covers claims made against a director based on what she has done wrong as a director. The big difference between the two forms of insurance is that the insurance companies selling D & O insurance don't use Chris Paul or Flo or a gecko as their spokesperson.

Both automobile insurance policies and D & O insurance policies are contracts. The relevant law governing each is primarily contract law. Your exam will not (or at least should not) ask questions about contract law—only questions about business associations/organizations law.

All that business associations/organizations law has to say about D & O insurance is that (1) the Delaware General Corporations Statute, the MBCA, and other state corporations statutes permit corporations to purchase D & O insurance and (2) the limitations on indemnification discussed below do not apply to insurance. Again, the question of whether a director is protected by D & O insurance is a question of contract law—not one of your exam questions.

2. Why Are the Three Statutory Categories of Indemnification Important?

Just as all states authorize corporations to buy D & O insurance, all states have statutory provisions that authorize corporations to reimburse directors for litigation costs. These statutory provisions—typically referred to as indemnification statutes—typically create three categories. Three!

I emphasize three even though the MBCA only has two relevant sections: a section entitled "Permissible Indemnification", MBCA 8.51 and a section entitled "Mandatory Indemnification", MBCA section 8.52. Reading more than the titles of the MBCA and the Delaware General Corporation Statute reveals three different categories of indemnification.

Category (1) Mandatory Indemnification

A corporation must indemnify a director who was "wholly successful" in the litigation. If the court rules for the defendant director, then the corporation must reimburse the director for the litigation expenses she incurred. Just that simple. The only possible legal issue is what does "wholly successful" mean.

"Wholly successful", a phrase used both by the MBCA and the Delaware General Corporation Statute, means a judgment in the director's favor, regardless of the reason for the judgment. Winning on a motion to dismiss because the plaintiff lacked standing to bring a derivative action or on a motion for summary judgment because the statute of limitations has run is just as "wholly successful" as a jury verdict on the merits.

"Wholly." The win must be a total win. No mandatory indemnification for the director defendant who was sued by a plaintiff seeking $1,000,000 and receiving only a judgment of $1. The $1 judgment for the plaintiff is not "wholly successful" for the director defendant.

Similarly, the statutes do not mandate indemnification if the director settles. Settling a $1,000,000 lawsuit for $1 is not "wholly successful."

Corporations "may" (not "shall") still indemnify directors who are not "wholly successful"—so long as the indemnification statutes do not prohibit indemnification. So let's next learn when indemnification is prohibited.

Category (2) Prohibited Indemnification

Prohibited indemnification fact patterns involve shareholder derivative actions. If the plaintiff is the corporation or a shareholder bringing a derivative suit on behalf of the corporation, the corporation is prohibited from indemnifying the director *for any judgment or amount paid in settlement where the payment goes to the corporation*. To illustrate, P, an Acme Corp. shareholder, brings a shareholder derivative suit against D, a director of Acme Corp., alleging D's breach of their fiduciary duty caused Acme Corp. to lose $200,000. D settles for $99,000. If D paid the $99,000 settlement to Acme Corp. and Acme Corp. was able to indemnify D by reimbursing D for the $99,000 that D paid to Acme Corp., then the litigation and the settlement would have been pointless.

Note that I italicized the words "for any judgment or amount paid in settlement." The absolute prohibition on indemnification is limited to the judgment or amount in settlement. The prohibition on indemnification does not include reimbursement of the defendant director's attorneys' fees or other litigation-related expenses unless (i) the defendant director was "adjudged liable" and (ii) received an "improper financial benefit." MBCA 8.51(d)(2).

Category (3) Permissive Indemnification

This is the residual category. If indemnification is neither mandated nor prohibited, then it is permitted.

The above shareholder derivative suit hypothetical provides an example of permissive indemnification. D's attorneys' fees and other litigation expenses incurred in P's derivative suit on behalf of Acme Corp. come within category 3 permissive indemnification.

This direct suit hypothetical provides another example of permissive indemnification: S, a shareholder, sues the board of directors of Baker Corp. alleging that they had been wrongfully denied access to Baker Corp's books and records. Baker Corp's board of directors pays $100,000 to S to settle the direct suit and incurs attorneys' fees of $20,000. Both the $100,000 settlement payment and the $20,000 expenses come within category 3 permissive indemnification.

Did you pick up on the difference in what comes within permissible indemnification in direct actions from what comes within permissible indemnification in derivative actions? As to direct actions, judgments and amounts paid in settlements, as well as expenses, come within the category of permissible indemnification. As to derivative actions, only expenses come within the category of permissible indemnification and then only if (i) there was not a judgment for the plaintiff and (ii) no "financial benefit" to the director.

Moreover, indemnification statutes further limit indemnification for category three permissive indemnification to directors who can show that they (1) acted in good faith and (2) with the reasonable belief that they acted in the best interests of the corporation.

3. How Do the Articles of Incorporation Further Protect a Director from Bearing the Financial Consequences of Breach of Fiduciary Duty?

The articles of incorporation can protect a director from bearing the financial consequences of a breach of fiduciary duty in two different ways. First, the articles of incorporation can in essence combine the first and third categories of indemnification by requiring the corporation to reimburse any director who meets the requirements for permissive indemnification. Second, as you read in Chapter 17 the articles of incorporation can eliminate liability for breach of duty of care.

CHAPTER 20

What You Need to Know About Dividends and Other Distributions to Shareholders

Money. Generally, the reason that a person buys stock is to make money. One way that a stockholder makes money from his purchase of stock is receiving cash dividends from the corporation.

You need to know five things about cash dividends: (1) how does a corporation's paying cash dividends affect its balance sheet, (2) what determines whether a corporation *can* pay cash dividends to its shareholders, (3) who decides whether cash dividends *will* be paid, (4) to whom will the dividends be paid, and (5) the differences, if any, between cash dividends and "distributions."

1. How Does a Corporation's Paying Cash Dividends Affect Its Balance Sheet?

Recall that one side of a corporation's balance sheet has the corporation's cash and other assets, and the other side has both the corporation's debts and its equity. The two sides must balance. Saying the same thing another way: Assets - Debts = Equity.

A corporation's paying cash to its shareholders reduces the asset side of the balance sheet. It does not reduce debts; it reduces equity.

To illustrate, Acme Corp. has assets of 100, debts of 20 and equity of 80. If Acme Corp. distributes cash dividends totaling 30 to its shareholder, that would (1) reduce assets from 100 to 70, (2) leave the 20 of debt unaffected, and (3) reduce equity from 80 to 50. And, the balance sheet still balances.

2. What Determines Whether a Corporation *Can* Pay Cash Dividends to Its Shareholders?

Loan agreements and state corporation statutes determine whether a corporation *can* pay cash dividends to its shareholders.

Loan agreements commonly prohibit a debtor corporation from paying cash dividends to its shareholders until the debt is repaid. That is just contract law and so does not show up on BA/BO exams.

It is the state corporation statutes' prohibitions that commonly appear on exams. So, let's understand the state corporation statutes.

Remember that debt comes before/above equity in a balance sheet—i.e., rights of creditors come above/before rights of shareholders. Creditors also come before shareholders in state corporation statutes.

Corporation statutes protect creditors by imposing limitations on whether a corporation can pay cash dividends to its shareholders—i.e., limitations that are intended to ensure that the corporation will still be able to pay its creditors after paying the cash dividends to its shareholders.

The form of such creditor protection provided by the MBCA is very different from the form of protection provided by the Delaware

General Corporation Statute. In the unlikely event that your prof covered the dividends statutes in detail, I have provided a detailed explanation of each statute.

MBCA 6.40 has a two-part test, and a corporation's payment of a cash dividend is proper only if it meets *both* parts. Under the MBCA, a corporation is prohibited from paying cash dividends if, thereafter, either (1) the corporation will be unable to pay its debts as they become due in the ordinary course of business *or* (2) the value of the corporation's assets will be less than the amount of its debts plus the amount needed to pay to liquidation preferences. It's (2) you need to look out for on an exam, and so let's use the following hypothetical to look at (2) more carefully.

Assume that Acme Corp. has Class A stock and Class B stock and that Class B stock has a $2 liquidation preference. That means that if Acme Corp. liquidates and pays its creditors in full, then each share of Class B stock must receive $2 before the Class A shares get anything. And it means that if Acme Corp has $50,000 of assets, $40,000 of debts and 1,000 outstanding shares of Class B stock, under the MBCA, Acme Corp could not declare dividends of more than $8,000 = $50,000 - [$40,000 + (1,000 × 2)].

Again, the MBCA has a two-part test and a corporation can pay cash dividends only if it meets both parts of the test.

Delaware section 173 has a very different two-part test. A corporation can pay cash dividends if it meets either part: (1) A corporation can pay cash dividends from its net profits for the current fiscal year and/or from its net profits of the prior fiscal year (thus, if Acme Corp. has net profits of $100,000 in 2025 and net profits of $200,000 in 2026, it could pay cash dividends of up to $300,000); *or* (2) even if Acme Corp. was not profitable in either 2025 or 2026 it could pay cash dividends in 2026 up to the amount of its "surplus."

With the Delaware statutory restrictions on cash dividends, as with the MBCA restrictions on cash dividends, once again, it is (2) that you need to look out for on an exam. Especially the word "surplus" as used in the Delaware statute.

"Surplus" as a permissible source of dividends under the Delaware dividend statute is assets minus (debts + stated capital). Saying the same thing another way, a Delaware corporation can pay cash dividends to its shareholders under (2) only if, after the dividends have been paid, the amount of the corporation's post-dividend assets is greater than the amount of the corporation's debts plus the amount of the corporation's stated capital.

You should already know what assets and debts are. You now need to know what "stated capital" is. Knowing what "stated capital" is requires remembering what "par value" is. Look at the next hypothetical to remember what par value is and to understand what "stated capital" is.

Assume that Acme Corp. has assets of 100 and debts of 20. Acme Corp. has issued 30 shares of $1 par stock. You need to know three things about Acme's 30 outstanding shares of $1 par stock.

First, you need to know that the stock is $1 par only if that is what Acme's certificate of incorporation provides. Acme's certificate of incorporation could have provided that the par value was $200 a share; it could have provided that the par value of a share was 3 cents a share; it could have provided that the stock had no par value, i.e., "no par stock."

Second, you need to know that par value is important because it is the minimum issuance price. Acme Corp. must have received consideration with a value of $1 for each share it has issued. Since Acme Corp. has issued 30 shares of $1 par stock, Acme must have received consideration with a value of at least $30.

Again, par value is a minimum issuance price—not a fixed price. Acme Corp. can issue a share of $1 par stock for more than $1 or other consideration with a value of more than $1.

Third, you need to know that par value is also important because it establishes the minimum amount of a corporation's stated capital. Since Acme Corp. has issued 30 shares of $1 par stock, it has a minimum stated capital of at least $30.

Each time Acme Corp. issues a share of $1 par stock, then at least $1 is treated as stated capital. If Acme Corp. issues $1 par stock for more than $1, the Acme board of directors has the opportunity, but not the obligation, to allocate more than $1 of the issuance price to stated capital. For example, Acme Corp. could have issued the 30 shares of $1 stock for consideration totaling $400 and allocated all $400 to stated capital.[1]

Assuming that Acme Corp. has only allocated to stated capital the $1 par value for each of the 30 shares it has issued, then its stated capital would be $30. Under our other facts—assets of $100 and debts of $20, Acme Corp. could legally distribute no more than $50 in cash dividends: (100 - (20 + 30)).

To review the Delaware statutory restrictions on a corporation's paying cash dividends to its shareholders, dividends are permitted if the corporation meets *either* the assets minus debt plus stated capital test explained above, or the net profits from the current and/or past fiscal year test discussed above. Dividends paid out of such net profits by a corporation that has no "surplus" are commonly referred to as "nimble dividends."

---

1 You might ask "what is the stated capital for a Delaware corporation that has issued only no par stock"? On reflection, that seems more like a question that your professor might ask. Regardless of who asks the question, the answer is that the board of directors has complete discretion. If Baker Corp. issues 70 shares of no par stock for $800,000, the Baker Corp. board of directors can decide to allocate $800,000 or $2 or 0 to stated capital.

3. Who Decides Whether Cash Dividends Will Be Paid??

State corporation statutes answer the question of when a corporation *can* pay cash dividends to its shareholders. However, state corporation statutes do not even consider the question of when an eligible corporation *must* pay cash dividends to its shareholders. Saying the same thing another way, shareholders have no statutory rights to cash dividends.

Similarly, state courts do not consider the related question of when an eligible corporation should pay cash dividends to its shareholders. Case law does not recognize a common law right to cash dividends.

It is the board of directors that makes the decision of when and how much of a cash dividend is to be paid to shareholders.

That is consistent with what you have already learned about corporate decision-making. The board of directors makes decisions. Courts do not generally review the merits of the board's decisions unless the plaintiff challenging the decision can establish an exception to the business judgment rule, such as lack of good faith.

Zidell v. Zidell, a case appearing in business associations/ organizations casebooks, is illustrative. The trial court there had ordered the corporation to increase dividend payments. The Oregon Supreme Court reversed on the grounds that (1) judicial review of the merits of the board's dividends decisions was limited by the business judgment rule and (2) the plaintiff did not meet his burden of proving a lack of good faith to overcome the business judgment rule. In so ruling, the court notes plausible business reasons for a corporation's not paying cash dividends to its shareholders.[2]

---

[2] "Defendants introduced a considerable amount of credible evidence to explain their conservative dividend policy. There was testimony that the directors took into consideration a future need for expensive physical improvements and

Many casebooks also include *Dodge v. Ford Motor Co.*, the only reported case ordering a corporation to pay dividends. Since this is a case with unique facts, you need to be prepared to distinguish the facts of any exam question from the facts in *Dodge v. Ford Motor Co.*

The critical fact in *Dodge v. Ford Motor Co.* was the defendant's failure to give the court a business reason for Ford Motor Co.'s not declaring dividends. Instead of offering any one of a number of plausible business reasons for Ford Motor Co.'s not declaring dividends, the defendant Henry Ford testified that improving the lot of the working man by selling cars for less was the reason for not paying cash dividends to the Dodge brothers and other Ford shareholders. In essence, judicial review of the merits of the decision was not precluded by the business judgment rule because the defendant did not explain the dividends decision as a decision made because of a business judgment.

4. To Whom Does the Corporation Pay Cash Dividends?

Dividends are paid to the record owner as of the record date. Unless the board of directors otherwise orders, the record date is the date that the board authorized the dividend payments.

Remember that a corporation's articles can provide for multiple classes of stock, with some classes that have preferences when it comes to dividends. Such stock is referred to as "preferred stock."

---

possibly even the relocation of a major plant; the need for cash to pay for large inventory orders; the need for renovation of a nearly obsolescent dock; and the need for continued short term financing through bank loans which could be 'called' if the corporations' financial position became insecure. There was also evidence that earnings for 1973 and 1974 were abnormally high because of unusual economic conditions that could not be expected to continue."

Answering the question to whom does the corporation pay dividends requires you to understand not just the term "preferred" but also the terms "participating" and "cumulative."

"Preferred" simply means paid first. It does not necessarily mean paid the most.

To illustrate, Acme Corp. has issued 100 shares of Class A common stock and a 100 shares of Class B preferred stock that has $2 dividend preference. Acme's board decides to pay cash dividends totaling $1,000. Here is how that $1,000 would be allocated. First, $2 would be allocated to each Class B share. Preferred means paid first, and a $2 dividend preference means that $2 a share must be paid to Class B stockholders before anything is paid to Class A stockholders. After paying $200 ($2 × 100) to the Class B preferred shares, there would still be $800 to be paid to the 100 shares of Class A common stock. In this hypothetical, the common stock would receive a larger dividend—$8 a share—than the preferred—$2 a share. And, that is a possibility[3]—unless the Class B stock is not only "preferred" as to dividends, but also "participating."

If a corporation's articles provide for a class that is both preferred and participating, that class both gets paid its dividend preference first and also gets paid again with the common from whatever is left. Such a class of stock is called "participating" because it, in essence, "participates" with the common.

To illustrate, Acme Corp. has issued 100 shares of Class A common stock and a 100 shares of Class B preferred stock that has $2 dividend preference and is also participating. Acme's board decides to pay cash dividends totaling $1,000. Here is how that $1,000 would be allocated. First, $2 would be allocated to each Class B share. Again, preferred means paid first, and a $2 dividend

[3] But only a possibility. If the Acme board had decided to pay dividends totaling $300, then each Class B preferred share would get $2 and each Class A common share would get only $1. Preferred would have been both paid first and paid the most.

preference means that is $2 a share that must be paid first to the Class B stockholders. After paying $200 ($2 × 100) to the Class B preferred shares, there would still be $800 to be distributed to each of the 100 Class A common shares and the 100 Class B preferred and participating shares. Thus each Class A share would receive $4—$800 divided by (100 + 100)—and each Class B share would receive another $4 for a total of $6 a share.

The last word to watch for in exam questions on payment of cash dividends is "cumulative." Understanding the importance of a corporation's articles of incorporation providing that a class of stock is not only preferred but also cumulative requires you to remember two previously covered dividends concepts.

First, a corporation might be prohibited by statute from declaring dividends in a particular year. Dividends on preferred stock just like dividends on common stock cannot violate the statutory restrictions on dividends.

Second, even if a corporation is statutorily eligible to pay cash dividends, the board of directors can decide against paying cash dividends. Having preferred stock does not guarantee the shareholder a dividend each year.

Accordingly, it is possible that there will be years in which holders of preferred stock do not receive any dividend. Because of this possibility, it is common for a corporation's articles of incorporation to provide for a class of stock that is both preferred and "cumulative." If the articles so provide and the corporation fails to pay a dividend, the missed dividend "accumulates."

To illustrate, Baker Corp.'s Class C stock has a $2 dividend preference and is cumulative. Baker Corp. fails to pay a dividend for 3 years. When Baker Corp declares a dividend, Class C shares would get $8—$2 for the current year + ($2 × 3) for the 3 missed years—before any dividend payment to the common stock.

5. What Is the Difference Between Cash Dividend and "Distribution"?

The MBCA uses the term "distribution," not cash dividend. The MBCA definition of "distribution" includes cash dividends. Under the MBCA, cash dividends are one form of distribution—but only one form.

The other exam-important form of MBCA "distribution" is a corporation's repurchase of its shares from its shareholders. To illustrate, Acme Corp. has 1,000 shares outstanding. Acme Corp. used $600 of its assets to repurchase 200 of its shares from shareholders for $3 a share. Under the MBCA, Acme's repurchasing its shares is a "distribution," just as a cash dividend is a "distribution."

Compare the consequences of each. In each, the corporation is transferring its assets to its shareholders. The balance sheet consequences of each is a reduction in the corporation's assets and a corresponding reduction in equity. The amount of the corporation's debt is unchanged, but there will be less assets available to satisfy that debt.

Consequently, under the MBCA, a corporation's purchasing shares from its shareholders is subject to the same statutory limitations as the corporation's paying a cash dividend to its shareholders.

A stock dividend, however, is not a "distribution." It is not even really a dividend.

Think about the financial consequences of Acme's board of directors declaring a stock dividend—e.g., issuing an additional 200 shares as a stock dividend. The existence of additional 200 outstanding shares would have no effect on Acme's balance sheet and no effect on Acme's creditors. Under the MBCA, stock dividends are not subject to the same restrictions as cash dividends and other distributions.

CHAPTER 21

What You Need to Know About Close Corporations

You need to know three things about close corporations: (1) the definition (or lack of a definition) of a close corporation, (2) the legal protection for minority shareholders of close corporations, and (3) the previously covered legal concepts applicable only to close corporations.

1. What Is a Close Corporation?

A close corporation is kind of like porn. In determining what is a close corporation, courts use a "know it when I see it"[1] approach instead of a generally accepted legal definition.

Neither the MBCA nor the corporation statutes of most states contain a definition of "close corporation." The Delaware General Corporation Statute does contain a definition of "close corporations," but that is relevant only if the close corporation was

[1] *Cf.* http://blogs.wsj.com/law/2007/09/27/the-origins-of-justice-stewarts-i-know-it-when-i-see-it/; but *cf.* http://www.history.com/topics/us-presidents/george-bush/videos/youre-no-jack-kennedy.

incorporated in Delaware. A close corporation generally does not incorporate in Delaware unless its business is based in Delaware.

Some state court judges and law professors have attempted to be more helpful in explaining what a "close corporation" is than Justice Potter Stewart was in explaining what porn is in his *Jacobellis* opinion. Different courts and commentators provide different descriptions of a "close corporation."

None of these descriptions of a "close corporation" focus on the size of the corporation's business or the number of outstanding shares of the corporation's stock. Instead, in describing close corporations judges and law professors focus on two factors: (1) the number of shareholders the corporation has and (2) the market difficulty a shareholder encounters in selling her shares.

As to the first factor—number of shareholders—there is no "magic number" in the case law. However, in exam hypotheticals, look for a corporation with 30 or fewer shareholders—that is the maximum number of shareholders in the Delaware General Corporation Statute's definition of "close corporation."

The second factor—market difficulty in reselling shares—almost inevitably follows from the first. It is important to understand that the difficulty in selling shares is created by the lack of a market, not by rules of law.

Recall from Chapter 8, the legal difficulty that a partner encounters in trying to sell their partnership interest. State partnership statutes limit what a partner can sell to third parties to what statutes call the "transferable interest."

There are no similar statutory limitations on a shareholder's selling her shares. In theory, a shareholder's interest in the corporation, i.e., their stock, is freely transferable.

In reality, a shareholder's interest in a corporation like McDonald's that has millions of shareholders and a market for its stock is freely transferable. If (for whatever bizarre reason you can imagine) McDonald's is not treating one of its shareholders fairly, she can easily sell their shares.

There is a different reality for a shareholder in a close corporation, such as Acme Corporation, which has three shareholders. In theory, Acme Corporation stock is just as freely transferable as McDonald's stock. In reality, it is not. While more than five million shares of McDonald's stock are sold on a typical day, there typically has been no sales of the stock of a close corporation like Acme Corporation since the three shareholders bought their shares from the corporation.

Why then would anyone ever buy stock in a close corporation? It is easy to see the primary reason that millions of people buy shares in a large, publicly traded corporation like McDonald's—they hope to later resell those shares at a profit.

It is not as easy to see the reasons that people buy stock in a close corporation. People do not buy stock in close corporations in order to resell their shares at a profit. People buy stock in close corporations for different reasons.

The most common reason that a person buys stock in a close corporation is employment opportunities. Assume for example, that Archie, Ken, and Wanda are unhappy with their jobs. They decide to get into the jewelry business as a new line of work. Archie, Ken, and Wanda form a corporation, Goldfish, Inc. (GI). They become both the shareholders and employees of GI, which owns and operates the jewelry business.

A less common reason that a person buys stock in a close corporation is dividend opportunities. Otto may buy stock in GI because he believes that GI will be profitable and he wants to share in GI's profits by receiving stock dividends.

In a close corporation, a shareholder who does not own a majority of the stock may be in a very precarious investment position. The other shareholders might decide not to hire them or decide to terminate their employment. The other shareholders might decide to increase their salaries or expand the business, instead of paying dividends.

A minority shareholder in a close corporation can be stuck with stock that brings no return on investment. As we will see in the next section, courts—especially courts in Massachusetts—have been increasingly willing to step in and create common law concepts to protect minority stockholders of close corporations from oppression.

2. How Do Courts Protect Minority Shareholders of a Close Corporation?

Massachusetts' courts have taken the lead in protecting minority shareholders of a close corporation. Massachusetts is to exam questions about closely held corporations, what Delaware is to exam questions about publicly traded corporations.

The seminal Massachusetts close corporations case, a case included in most business associations/business organizations casebooks, is *Donahue v. Rodd Electrotype Co.* Donahue had been an employee and minority shareholder in a close corporation, largely owned and operated by Harry Rodd[2] and his children.

Donahue's widow inherited the 50 shares of the corporation that had been issued to Donahue. The other 198 shares were owned by Harry and his children.

Harry wanted to retire but also wanted financial security. The three-person board of directors of the corporation—two of whom were Harry's sons—agreed that the corporation would buy 45 of

2 Real name—honest!

Harry's shares at $800 per share (indicated to be the book and liquidating value of the shares).

Donahue then tendered her 50 shares to the corporation, offering to sell them at the same price. The corporation refused, and she sued, alleging breach of fiduciary duty to a minority stockholder.

The lower courts ruled for defendants, and concluded that the purchase of Harry's stock was done in good faith. The Supreme Judicial Court of Massachusetts reversed, and established the "equal access" rule.

The "equal access" rule is simple enough: controlling shareholders of a close corporation owe a fiduciary duty to minority shareholders to accord them an equal opportunity to sell their stock to the corporation. The holding is limited to close corporations, which the court defines as having: (1) a small number of shareholders; (2) no ready market for its stock; and (3) substantial majority shareholder participation in management.

Because Rodd Electrotype Co. comes within this definition of a close corporation, the equal access rule applies. Under the equal access rule, the corporation must either buy Donahue's stock at $800 per share or rescind the purchase of Harry's stock.

In reaching that result, the majority in *Donahue* used very broad language equating a close corporation with a partnership: "we hold that stockholders in the close corporation owe one another substantially the same fiduciary duty in the operation of the enterprise that partners owe to one another." Even though the court uses the phrase "we hold," this statement is dictum.

The court in *Donahue* was deciding whether the corporation's purchase of Harry's stock was a breach of a fiduciary duty. The board of directors of Rodd Electrotype Co., not the majority shareholders of Rodd Electrotype Co, made the decision to buy Harry's stock.[3]

More problematic is the Massachusetts Supreme Judicial Court's statement in *Donahue* that majority shareholders must always subordinate their interests to the interests of the minority: "They may not act out of avarice, expediency or self-interest in derogation of their duty of loyalty to other shareholders. . . ."

In a later Massachusetts case, *Wilkes v. Springside Nursing Home, Inc.*, the minority shareholder plaintiff, like the minority shareholder plaintiff in *Donahue*, prevailed on his breach of fiduciary duty claim. Nonetheless, the *Wilkes* opinion represents at least a retreat from the broad duty imposed on the majority shareholders of close corporations in the *Donahue* majority opinion.

In *Wilkes*, the Massachusetts Supreme Judicial Court both (i) relied on *Donahue* reasoning and (ii) backed away from the above *Donahue* language. The court in *Wilkes* stated "The majority, concededly, has certain rights to what has been termed 'selfish ownership' in the corporation." More specifically, the *Wilkes* court recognized that there might be a legitimate business reason for discriminating among shareholders in a close corporation.

The case involved employment for shareholders of a close corporation. Wilkes was one of the four original shareholders of Springside Nursing Home, Inc. and also one of the four original members of the board of directors. For a time, all of the shareholders worked at the nursing home and received a salary.

Because of what the court described as "deterioration in his personal relationship with his associates," the board of directors

---

[3] I understand that the majority shareholders of Rodd Electrotype Co. and the majority of the directors of Rodd Electrotype Co. are the same people. And, you understand that when a director makes a contested decision, a court in resolving that contest looks to the law relating to directors, regardless of whether that person is also a shareholder.

later decided that the corporation should stop paying Wilkes a salary.[4] Wilkes sued alleging breach of fiduciary duty.

In holding for the plaintiff Wilkes, the court reasoned:

(i) stockholders in a close corporation owe one another a "fiduciary duty";

(ii) when a plaintiff minority shareholder brings a suit alleging a breach of "the strict good faith duty," the defendant controlling shareholder group must show a "legitimate business purpose" for its action;

(iii) even if the defendant makes such a showing, the plaintiff still prevails if he can show that the defendant could have met its legitimate business purpose in some other, less oppressive way.

Recall that the defendants terminated Wilkes because "deterioration in his personal relationship with his associates"—not a "legitimate business purpose."

Cases in several other states have relied on these Massachusetts cases to find that shareholders of a close corporation owe each other a fiduciary duty the same as the duty of a partner to her fellow partners. In *Nixon v. Blackwell,* Delaware expressly rejected special fiduciary duties protecting minority shareholders of close corporations, but more states have looked to Massachusetts close corporations case law than to Delaware close corporations case law.

---

[4] Note that the challenged decision in *Wilkes*—termination of Wilkes' employment—like the challenged action in *Donahue*—buying Harry's stock but not Donahue's—was a decision by the board of directors. Generally, decisions by the board of directors are protected by the business judgment rule, UNLESS THERE IS A CONFLICT OF INTEREST and there was a conflict of interest in both *Donahue* and *Wilkes*.

3. Which Previously Considered Corporate Law Concepts Are Applicable Only to Close Corporations?

Six previously considered corporate law concepts are applicable only to close corporations.

First, shareholder agreements as to how a corporation can be managed (page 107, supra). Under MBCA 7.32, all of the shareholders can agree in writing to eliminate the board of directors or limit the decision-making of the board of directors.

An agreement by all shareholders that there be no board of directors makes sense for a close corporation, such as our hypothetical Goldfish, Inc. jewelry store with its three shareholders, all of whom work for the corporation. Hard to imagine a board of directors meeting at Goldfish, Inc. jewelry store.

However, such an MBCA 7.32 agreement makes no sense for a public corporation like McDonald's. It is hard to imagine all of the millions of shareholders of a public corporation like McDonald's agreeing to anything—much less agreeing to eliminate the board of directors.

Second, cumulative voting (page 97). Under both the Delaware General Corporation Statute and the MBCA, shareholders can use cumulative voting in voting for directors if the articles of incorporation expressly so provide. While neither the Delaware General Corporation Statute nor the MBCA expressly so provides, the use of cumulative voting is limited to close corporations.

Third, preemptive rights (page 88). Similarly, under both the Delaware General Corporation statute and the MBCA, shareholders have a right to maintain their percentage of ownership by buying their proportionate interest on any new offerings, if the articles of incorporation expressly so provide. And, again, while neither the Delaware General Corporation Statute nor the MBCA expressly so provides, the use of preemptive rights is limited to close corporations.

Fourth and fifth, voting agreements and voting trusts (pages 100–101). Both the Delaware General Corporation Statute and the MBCA expressly authorize shareholders to agree about how their shares are to be voted by using either a voting trust or a voting agreement. And, yet again, while neither the Delaware General Corporation Statute nor the MBCA expressly so provides, the use of voting trusts and voting agreements is limited to close corporations.

Sixth, piercing the corporate veil (pages 79–83). While generally shareholders are not liable for the debts of their corporation, courts have created a common law exception generally referred to as piercing the corporate veil. All of the reported piercing the corporate veil cases involve close corporations.

CHAPTER 22

What Do You Need to Know About the Legal Obligations of Shareholders to the Corporation?

This is a really, really short chapter. This is a really, really short chapter because (i) there is not much you need to know about the legal obligations of shareholders to the corporation and (ii) we have already covered most of it.

Generally, a shareholder does not owe any legal obligation to the corporation whose shares he owns. Even though you own stock in Yumi Brands, Inc which owns Kentucky Fried Chicken, it is okay (probably better than "okay") for you to buy fried chicken nuggets from Chic-fil-A instead of KFC. What is more is likely to be tested by your BA prof is that a shareholder does not breach any fiduciary duty by neglecting to vote his shares, by voting his shares while uninformed, by voting his shares in the way that he thinks will harm the corporation.

There are three generally recognized exceptions to the general rule that a shareholder does not owe any legal obligation to the corporation. We have already encountered the first two of three exceptions.

1. What is the Managing Shareholder Exception to the General Rule That a Shareholder Does Not Owe any Legal Obligation to the Corporation Whose Shares He Owns?

You were introduced to one of the three exceptions in the last part of the last part of Chapter 16: "(6) If an MBCA section 7.32 shareholder agreement eliminates the board of directors so that shareholders, have the power of directors, these shareholders have the same "liability for acts and omissions imposed by law on directors."

For example, if Larry, Moe, Curly, Shemp and Joe are the only shareholders of TS Inc and all five agree that (i) TS Inc will not have a board of directors and (ii) Larry can make the decisions for TS Inc that usually would be made by a board of directors, then Larry has all of the same legal obligations to the corporation that a director would have. Some B.A. profs will call Larry a "managing shareholder."

2. What is the Close Corporation Exception to the to the General Rule That a Shareholder Does Not Owe Any Legal Obligation to the Corporation Whose Shares He Owns?

There are some obvious factual similarities between the typical close corporation and the typical partnership, starting with that both the typical close corporation and the typical partnership have relatively owners who informally make the decisions for the business entity. And, we have seen in Chapter 21, courts in Massachusetts and a number of other states have imputed the fiduciary concepts that apply to the partners in a partnerships to the shareholders of a corporation with relatively few shareholders, i.e., a close corporation.

While these cases talk about the fiduciary duty of all shareholders of a close corporation, the facts of the cases focus on action taken by a majority shareholder or a group of shareholders holding a majority of the shares. On your exam, watch for a fact pattern in which a corporation with relatively few shareholders takes some action that harms a minority shareholder or benefits only a majority shareholder or a group of shareholders holding a majority of the shareholders and acting in concert[1].

3. What is the Controlling Shareholder Exception to the General Rule That a Shareholder Does Not Owe Any Legal Obligation to the Corporation Whose Shares He Owns?

We know that if D is both a shareholder and also a director then when D acts as a director D has legal obligations to the corporation whose shares D owns. To revisit the example in Chapter 17, if D is a shareholder and member of the board of directors of BBC corporation and the owner of Redacre, D's sale of Redacre to BBC would be subject to the legal obligations of "interested director transactions" discussed in Chapter 17.

Don't remember those legal obligation discussed in the Chapter 17 materials on interested director transactions? D faces liability to BBC unless D can establish that either (i) the transaction was approved by a majority of disinterested directors or the disinterested holders of a majority of the shares that approved

[1] This is probably my last book, and I have always wanted to use the phrase "acting in concert." Cf https://www.youtube.com/watch?v=xqC2BXeJrUE

BBC's purchase of Redacre after full disclosure or (2) the "entire fairness" of the transaction to BBC.

What if D is a BBC shareholder and the owner of Redacre but not a BBC director? Some cases that appear in most Business Associations casebooks such as *Sinclair Oil Corp. v, Levien* and *Weinberger v. UOP, Inc* would treat D's sale of Redacre to BBC like an "interested director transaction" if D was a "controlling shareholder" at the time of the transaction.

In 2025, Delaware added a statutory definition of "controlling shareholder." An individual or a business entity is a "controlling shareholder" if he

(1) Owns enough shares to own shares with a majority of the "voting power[2]" OR

(2) Controls at least one third of the shares in terms of "voting power" together with the power to exercise managerial authority OR

(3) By contract or otherwise have the authority to cause the election of directors with majority "voting power"

---

[2] The Delaware statute looks to voting power instead of number of shares or number of directors because a corporation's articles can provide for classes of shares that have more than one vote per share and can provide for different votes for different directors

CHAPTER 23

What You Need to Know About Federal Securities Laws for a Basic Business Associations/ Organizations Course

Most law schools have an advanced course in Securities Regulation. Nonetheless, most business associations/organizations casebooks have materials on federal securities laws, and some professors cover that stuff, if your professor is one of that "some", then you should read this chapter.

The primary federal securities statutes are the Securities Act of 1933 ("33 Act") and the Securities Exchange Act of 1934 ("34 Act"). Advanced securities regulations courses cover those statutes and more.

In most basic BA/BO courses, the most important federal securities law is not a statutory provision. Instead, what is most important is an administrative regulation, Rule 10b-5—a rule promulgated by the Securities and Exchange Commission ("SEC") pursuant to section 10(b) of the 34 Act.

Most of what you need to know about Rule 10b-5 is how it applies to (1) a sale of a corporation's stock in which either the buyer or the seller relied on a false or misleading statement of material fact about the corporation and (2) a sale of a corporation's stock in which either the buyer or the seller relied on material nonpublic information about the corporation.

1. How Does Rule 10b-5 Come into Play When a Person Makes a False or Misleading Statement in Connection with a Stock Transaction?

Under state law, a person who buys stock as result of a false or misleading statement can invoke the common law concepts of misrepresentation, fraud and deceit. The contract law of misrepresentation was supposed to be covered and tested in your contracts course; the tort law of fraud and deceit was supposed to be covered and tested in your torts course. What was covered in your business associations/organizations course and will be tested on your BA/BO final is Rule 10b-5, and so let's learn Rule 10b-5 rather than relearning contracts or torts.

Rule 10b-5 prohibits making a false or misleading statement of material facts in connection with the purchase or sale of securities. If, for example, Ehrlich, one of three shareholders of California Gulf Sulfur, Inc. (CGS) who is neither an officer nor director of CGS induces Dinesh to buy his CGS stock by making false statements about mineral deposits on land owned by CGS, then Ehrlich has possibly violated Rule 10b-5.

Notice again that CGS only has three shareholders and that the wrongdoer Ehrlich is neither an officer nor a director. Rule 10b-5 applies to all sales of stock, regardless of who the seller and buyer are and regardless of whether the stock is stock of a public corporation like McDonald's or stock of a close corporation like CGS.

While the language of both Rule 10b-5 and section 10(b) is set out in a footnote below[1], most of what you need to know about Rule 10b-5 comes, not from the language of the 34 Act or of Rule 10b-5 itself, but from Supreme Court case law.

For example, Rule 10b-5 simply states "It shall be unlawful . . . to make an untrue statement of material fact . . . in connection with the purchase or sale of any security." These words suggest that the plaintiff in a Rule 10b-5 action must be the United States (either the Department of Justice or the SEC) and that all the United States has to prove is that: (i) the defendant made a statement in connection with the purchase or sale of stock; (ii) the statement was false; and (iii) the false statement was material.

Case law adds the following additional important information about possible plaintiffs. The plaintiff in a Rule 10b-5 case can be not only the United States but also the private party who bought or sold the stock.[2] Therefore, Dinesh can be a Rule 10b-5 plaintiff.

---

[1] Rule 10b-5: Employment of Manipulative and Deceptive Practices:

It shall be unlawful for any person, directly or indirectly, by the use of any means or instrumentality of interstate commerce, or of the mails or of any facility of any national securities exchange,

(a) To employ any device, scheme, or artifice to defraud,

(b) To make any untrue statement of a material fact or to omit to state a material fact necessary in order to make the statements made, in the light of the circumstances under which they were made, not misleading, or

(c) To engage in any act, practice, or course of business which operates or would operate as a fraud or deceit upon any person,

in connection with the purchase or sale of any security.

Section 10. Regulation of the Use of Manipulative and Deceptive Devices

It shall be unlawful . . .

(b) To use or employ in connection with the purchase or sale of any security . . . any manipulative or deceptive device. . . .

[2] *Blue Chip Stamps v. Manor Drug Stores*, 421 U.S. 723 (1975).

And (to sneak in a little bit of review), if Dinesh is the plaintiff in a Rule 10b-5 action, it will be a direct, not derivative, action. The claim belongs to Dinesh—he was the victim of Ehrlich's false statement.

Case law also adds information about what the plaintiff has to prove to prevail under Rule 10b-5. In addition to proving the falsity and materiality of Ehrlich's statement about the mineral deposits, Dinesh will also have to prove reliance and scienter.

Whether Ehrlich's statement about CGS's mineral deposits is false is a fact question and so not an exam issue. If Ehrlich's false statement about CGS's mineral deposits is on your exam, the three Rule 10b-5 issues that your prof will be looking for you to address are (1) materiality, (2) reliance, and (3) scienter.

1.1. Materiality

You need to know two things about materiality and Rule 10b-5. First, the general test for materiality: whether there is a substantial likelihood that a reasonable investor would consider the information important in deciding whether to buy or sell the stock. Don't worry about being able to apply this test. Just be able to paraphrase this test in your exam essay.

The second thing you need to know about materiality and Rule 10b-5 is the more specific *Basic, Inc. v. Levinson* test to determine materiality when the relevant facts are "contingent facts", i.e., something that may (but not necessarily will) happen.

In *Basic, Inc. v. Levinson*, Basic Inc. issued press releases denying that it was engaged in merger negotiations. These statements were false. Basic, Inc. was, in fact, secretly negotiating a merger at the time. When Basic, Inc. later announced the merger, a Rule 10b-5 class action was brought on behalf of people who sold their Basic, Inc. stock between the time of Basic, Inc.'s false denials and Basic Inc.'s merger announcement. The plaintiffs alleged that they received a lower price for their Basic, Inc. stock than they would have received if Basic, Inc. had not made false statements.

The Supreme Court in *Basic* adopted a sliding scale test for deciding the materiality of contingent facts, such as the potential but not yet actual merger, that considers (1) the magnitude of the possible event and (2) the probability that the event will occur. In other words, the greater the impact of the event, the less certain its occurrence must be in order for investors to find the information important and, thus, material.

Again, the *Basic* test is not the "basic test," i.e., the test that you generally apply. Again, the *Basic* test only becomes important when the false statement relates to "contingent facts."

1.2. Reliance

Think about what you can write concerning reliance in a fact pattern like Ehrlich's sale of stock to Dinesh. Not much. Your essay would simply state that (i) reliance is an element of a private cause of action under Rule 10b-5 and (2) Dinesh has the burden of proving reliance.

Reliance becomes more problematic in a fact pattern like *Basic, Inc. v. Levinson*, in which a class of plaintiffs is arguing that it relied on press releases. Should each member of the plaintiff class have to prove that they both read and relied on the false press releases in selling their shares of Basic, Inc.?

Instead of requiring any direct proof of reliance, the Court in *Basic* adopted what is called the "fraud on the market" theory.[3]

---

[3] The Court explained that "The fraud on the market theory is based on the hypothesis that, in an open and developed securities market, the price of a company's stock is determined by the available material information regarding the company and its business. . . . Misleading statements will therefore defraud purchasers of stock even if the purchasers do not directly rely on the misstatements. . . . The causal connection between the defendants' fraud and the plaintiffs' purchase of stock in

Basic's fraud on the market theory essentially eliminates a need to prove reliance when a public statement is made about a stock traded on a developed securities market such as the New York Stock Exchange.

1.3. Scienter

The Supreme Court has held that a Rule 10b-5 plaintiff must prove "scienter," which the Court then described as showing that the defendant acted with an intent to "deceive, manipulate or defraud." This precludes any Rule 10b-5 liability for any defendant who negligently mislead the buyer of her stock. While the Supreme Court made clear that there is no Rule 10b-5 liability for mere negligence, it left open the question of whether the plaintiff's proving that the defendant acted recklessly supports a Rule 10b-5 claim.

2. How Did the *Texas Gulf Sulphur* Case Expand the Application of Rule 10b–5 to "Insider Trading"?

We know from the language of Rule 10b-5(b) that saying stuff that is false (e.g., "Acme Corp. has been profitable every quarter" when Acme Corp. has not been profitable every quarter) or misleading (e.g., "Acme Corp. has been profitable every quarter" when the speaker knows that Acme will not be profitable this quarter) can be the basis for a Rule 10b-5 action by the government, or by the buyer, or seller of stock who relied on the false or misleading statement. *SEC v. Texas Gulf Sulphur Co.* was the first circuit court decision holding that the failure to say something, i.e., nondisclosure, can be the basis for a Rule 10b-5 action.

---

such a case is no less significant than in a case of direct reliance on misrepresentations."

Geologists acting for the Texas Gulf Sulphur Co. (TGS) found evidence of ore deposits on land TGS had optioned. TGS kept this information confidential—not even all of the members of the TGS board of directors knew of the mineral discovery—so that TGS could buy surrounding land cheaply.

Some TGS officers and directors, however, not only knew of the mineral findings but also (1) took advantage of this "material inside information" to buy TGS stock before the information became public and the price of TGS stock increased, and (2) "tipped," i.e., told others so that they could buy TGS stock before the information became public.[4]

The SEC filed a Rule 10b-5 action against (i) the officers and directors who bought TGS stock, (ii) the officers and directors who told others to buy TGS stock (now known as "tippers"), and (iii) non-insiders who were given this inside information (now known as "tippees").

The Second Circuit referred to the TGS officers and directors as "insiders" and held that these insiders violated Rule 10b-5 by "insider trading," i.e., buying TGS stock when they had material "inside information" (i.e., information unavailable to those with whom they were dealing). The Second Circuit also held that non-insiders, such as the people who had been told by insiders about the mineral find, violated Rule 10b-5 by buying TGS stock—"all transactions in TGS stock . . . by individuals apprised of the drilling results . . . were in violation of Rule 10b-5."

There is very broad dicta about insider trading in the Second Circuit's *Texas Gulf Sulphur* decision:

> "The essence of the Rule is that anyone who, trading for his own account in the securities of a corporation, has

---

[4] When they started buying, TGS stock was selling for $18 a share. In time, rumors started circulating and the price increased. At the time TGS announced its mineral discovery to the public, TGS stock was selling for $37 a share.

> '**access, directly or indirectly**, to information intended to be available only for a corporate purpose and not for the personal benefit of anyone' may not take 'advantage of such information knowing it is unavailable to those with whom he is dealing,' i.e., the investing public." (emphasis added)

Later Supreme Court decisions have in essence reduced the "essence of the Rule." While after *Texas Gulf Sulphur* it would seem that anyone in possession of material inside information about a corporation who bought or sold that corporation's stock violated Rule 10b-5, the Supreme Court in *Chiarella* and *Dirks* narrowed the impact of Rule 10b-5 on trading with inside information.

3. How Did Post-*Texas Gulf Sulphur* Supreme Court Decisions in *Chiarella* and *Dirks* Narrow the Impact of Rule 10b–5 on Trading with Inside Information?

In *Chiarella v. United States,* the person trading with the benefit of inside information was not an insider of the corporation whose stock he was purchasing. Instead, Chiarella worked for the printing company that was preparing tender offer documents. He was able to figure out the identity of the target corporation, bought its stock, and sold that stock for a profit after announcement of the tender offer.

Chiarella was convicted of violating Rule 10b-5. The Supreme Court reversed the conviction because the jury instruction was wrong.

The jury instruction was consistent with the above dicta from *Texas Gulf Sulphur*. The jury was told that all that they needed to find in order to convict Chiarella was that he benefitted from material, non-public information in buying the stock. The Supreme

Court held that the jury instruction was wrong—merely proving possession of material nonpublic information by a buyer of stock is not enough to establish a violation of Rule 10b-5.

In explaining this holding, the Court in *Chiarella* developed what has come to be known as the "traditional" or "classical theory" of insider trading. Under this theory, section 10(b) of the 34 Act and Rule 10b-5 are violated when a corporate insider with material nonpublic information buys or sells her corporation's stock. The violation arises from a breach of fiduciary duty. Directors and officers owe a fiduciary duty. Chiarella was an employee of an unrelated printed company, not a director or officer of the corporation's whose stock he purchased. Chiarella did not breach a fiduciary duty and so did not violate Rule 10b-5.[5]

Then in *Dirks v. SEC*, the Supreme Court limited the application of Rule 10b-5 with respect to tipping. Secrist, a *former* insider of Equity Funding Corporation (EFC), was concerned about fraud at EFC. Secrist tipped off Dirks, an investment analyst, to the EFC fraud in the hope that Dirks would expose the scheme.

Instead, Dirks told his brokerage firm's clients about the EFC fraud and they sold their EFC stock before the fraud became public knowledge, avoiding significant losses. The SEC censured Dirks for violating Rule 10b-5. The Supreme Court reversed.

In so ruling, the Court in *Dirks* provides three tipping rules:

(1) A person is a tipper for purposes of Rule 10b-5 only if she (i) is an insider of a corporation who (ii) passes along nonpublic information about the corporation (iii) in breach of a fiduciary duty to the corporation and (iv) receives some benefit for it. So Secrist was not a tipper. He received no benefit by revealing the

---

[5] After *Chiarella*, the SEC adopted Rule 14e-3 which bars everyone—not just directors and officers—from buying or selling stock on the basis of material, non-public information about tender offers.

information of the EFC fraud to Dirks, who was not a relative or friend[6].

(2) There cannot be a tippee for purposes of Rule 10b-5 without a tipper. Since Secrist was not a tipper, Dirks is not a tippee.

(3) A tippee assumes the fiduciary duty of his tipper, and so violates Rule 10b-5 by tipping others. Again, this does not apply to Dirks. Since Secrist violated no duty to EFC when he gave the information to Dirks, then Dirks did not violate Rule 10b-5 when he gave the same information to his firm's customers.

In footnote 14, the *Dirks* opinion suggests that accountants, attorneys, consultants, or underwriters who in the course of their work for a corporation receive non-public information should be viewed as temporary insiders with all the fiduciary obligations of an insider. Accordingly, such a person violates Rule 10b-5 by buying or selling stock of the corporation that she is working for, or by tipping others who buy or sell that stock.

4. How Does the *O'Hagan* "Misappropriation Theory" Expand the Insider Trading Application of Rule 10b–5?

In both *Chiarella* and *Dirks*, the Supreme Court focused on whether the defendant owed a fiduciary duty to the corporation whose stock was being bought or sold. In *O'Hagan*, the Court focused on whether the defendant owed a fiduciary duty to the source of the non-public information.

O'Hagan was a lawyer with a large firm. He learned of a tender offer that others in his firm were working on and bought stock in the

[6] In *Salman v. U.S.*, 580 U.S. 39 (2016), the Court said that tipping a relative or friend is a sufficient personal benefit.

target company, the Pillsbury Company. In a criminal proceeding, O'Hagan was convicted of violating section 10b of the 34 Act and Rule 10b-5. The Supreme Court affirmed the conviction.

O'Hagan was not a Pillsbury officer or director, nor did he receive material nonpublic information from a Pillsbury insider. Neither O'Hagan, nor his law firm was the attorney for Pillsbury. Accordingly, *O'Hagan* did not come within the classical or traditional theory of insider trading developed in *Chiarella* and *Dirks*.

The Court in *O'Hagan* did not rely on the classic theory of insider trading developed in *Chiarella* and *Dirks*. Instead, the *O'Hagan* case relied on the "misappropriation theory" of insider trading, which looks to the relationship between the defendant and the source of the nonpublic information.

The Court's reasoning was that O'Hagan was in a fiduciary relationship with his law firm and its clients. By buying stock of the target corporation, O'Hagan misappropriated information belonging to the law firm and its clients. This was a breach of his fiduciary duty, or, in the Court's language: "The misappropriation . . . was properly made the subject of a section 10(b) charge because it meets the statutory requirement that there be 'deceptive' conduct 'in connection with' securities transactions."

Two *O'Hagan* exam hints:

(1) The Supreme Court in *O'Hagan* expressly limits its use of the "misappropriation theory" to criminal actions.

(2) Footnote 14 from *Dirks* is not directly relevant to the *O'Hagan* facts. The Supreme Court's *O'Hagan* decision expands classical or traditional insider trading to lawyers working for the corporations whose stock they buy using material nonpublic

information. O'Hagan was not working for the target corporation whose stock he bought.

The Pillsbury Company[7], like Texas Gulf Sulphur Co. and the corporations involved in *Chiarella* and *Dirks*, was a large corporation. Remember, however, Rule 10b-5 applies to all corporations.

The other federal securities laws that might have been covered in your basic business associations/organizations course apply only to public corporations. Public corporations are, of course, corporations that have issued stock publicly. And, of course, a corporation's offering of its stock to the public is called a public offering.

5. How Do Federal Securities Laws Affect a Corporation's Issuance of Stock in a Public Offering?

Understanding how the federal securities laws affect a corporation's issuance of stock requires an understanding of the 33 Act's registration requirements and the 33 Act's exemptions from its registration requirements. Before attempting to understand the registration requirements, understand that the exemptions are so pervasive that comparatively few issuances of stock are subject to the 33 Act's registration requirements. In essence, registration is required only for public offerings and most stock issuances are not public offerings and so are exempt from the 33 Act's registration requirements.

These registration requirements are disclosure requirements. The 33 Act contemplates that a corporation issuing securities in a public offering will first file a detailed and extensive "registration

---

[7] Pillsbury—lots of dough, boy. *Cf.* https://www.youtube.com/watch?v=z_2RZABiePo.

statement" with the SEC. Then, the SEC reviews the adequacy of the information provided in the registration statement. Typically, the SEC will request changes.

After the issuing corporation has changed the registration statement as requested by the SEC, the issuing corporation provides a copy of the main part of the registration statement called the "prospectus" to all people to whom the corporation offers the securities. Offering stock to the public requires this extensive and expensive disclosure process.

Again, the 33 Act's registration requirements only apply to a corporation's issuance of stock to the public—a "public offering." Again, most corporations' issuances of stock come within the 33 Act's exemptions from these registration requirements. The most important factors in determining whether a corporation's issuance of stock is exempt from the 33 Act's registration requirements are (1) the number of people to whom the stock is being offered and (2) whether the issuer uses general advertising or otherwise engages in mass solicitation of offers.

Again, the 33 Act's registration requirements are in essence disclosure requirements. The SEC reviews the registration statement carefully for adequacy of information. The SEC does not pass on the substantive merits of the issuing corporation or the issuance.

6. What Does the Term "Registered Corporation" Mean?

Section 12 of the 34 Act requires corporations with shares traded on a national exchange, such as the New York Stock Exchange, or which have over $10,000,000 in assets and at least 500 shareholders who are not accredited investors to register with the SEC. These corporations are called "registered" or "34 Act companies." And, these corporations are subject to the proxy rules of section 14 of the 34 Act and the "short-swing trading" rules of section 16 of the 34 Act.

7. How Much Does a Student in a Basic Business Associations/Organizations Class Have to Know About the Federal Proxy Rules?

Hopefully, nothing. About 1/2 of the business associations/ organizations casebooks do not cover the federal proxy rules. And at least 1/2 of the professors who use casebooks with federal proxy rules materials do not cover that part of the book.

If your professor did cover the federal proxy rules, you need to know when you do state proxy law and when you do the federal proxy rule. The only likely exam question on state proxy laws will be a question about revocability of a proxy.

For example: If S grants a proxy to P and the proxy expressly states that it is irrevocable, can S still revoke the proxy? And, as you learned from page 95, S can still revoke unless there are other facts that show that this was a "proxy coupled with an interest."

For any question on the federal proxy rules, you also need to know five things about the federal proxy rules:

(1) registered corporations regularly solicit shareholder proxies to ensure that shareholder meeting quorum requirements are satisfied;

(2) these solicitations must be accompanied by a "proxy statement" which satisfies the requirements of the federal proxy rules;

(3) one such rule prohibits fraud in connection with the solicitation of a proxy;

(4) violation of this rule gives rise to a private right of action for damages; and

(5) a "qualified shareholder" can submit proposals for inclusion in the corporation's proxy solicitation materials.

The most likely exam question on federal proxy laws will involve a registered corporation's soliciting proxies from all of its shareholders to ensure that there will be a quorum and the necessary majority shareholder vote for the merger proposed by the board of directors.[8] A shareholder contends that the corporation's proxy statement was fraudulent.

In answering the question, you will need to point out

- Rule 14a-9 is a broad anti-fraud rule, covering both false statements of material facts and omissions of material facts;
- The test for materiality is "substantial likelihood that a reasonable shareholder would consider it important in deciding how to vote";[9]
- The Supreme Court has recognized an implied private right of action for violation of Rule 14a-9;
- In any such private right of action, shareholder reliance on the misstatement or omission in the proxy statement is presumed.[10]

---

[8] Or majority vote for the re-election of directors or majority vote on anything else requiring shareholder approval.

[9] *TSC Industries, Inc. v. Northway, Inc.*

[10] *Mills v. Electric Auto-Lite Co.*

The less likely question on federal proxy law will involve a registered corporation's refusing to include a shareholder proposal in a proxy statement. In answering the question, you will need to point out:

- whether the shareholder/proponent is eligible, i.e., whether the shareholder, for at least one year, has owned at least $2,000 or 1% (whichever is less) of the corporation's voting stock;
- whether one of the Rule 14a-8 restrictions on a shareholder's right to demand that a corporation include a proposal in its proxy statement is applicable.

8. How Does Section 16(b) of the 34 Act Discourage Insider Trading?

The 34 Act imposes additional disclosure requirements not only on registered corporations but also on the directors, officers, and ten percent shareholders of registered corporations. Under section 16(a) of the 34 Act, such persons must report to the SEC all of their purchases and sales of the corporation's stock within two business days of their occurrence. And, under section 16(b) any "profit" earned on purchases and sales within a six-month period must be disgorged to the corporation.

It can be difficult to prove that an insider who is buying or selling her corporation's stock is wrongly benefitting from material inside information—difficult to prove all of the elements of a Rule 10b-5 cause of action. By comparison, the elements of a cause of action under section 16(b) are easy to prove.

Section 16(b) provides a bright-line rule to discourage insiders from both buying and selling, or selling and buying, their corporation's stock within a six-month period. Any "section 16(b) profits" that the insider earns on such stock transactions must be forfeited to the corporation.

If your professor covered section 16(b) of the 34 Act, then you will need to know three things about section 16(b):

First: When do you apply section 16(b)?

Second: How do you apply section 16(b) to determine whether there is a profit as determined by section 16(b)?

Third: How is section 16(b) different from Rule 10b-5?

First: When do you apply section 16(b)?

Section 16(b) only applies when the stock being bought and sold is the stock of a registered corporation under the 34 Act. The same person must both buy stock of the corporation and sell stock of that corporation within a single six-month period. It does not matter which came first: buy then sell or sell then buy. The person buying and selling must be a 10% shareholder, or an officer or director.

The 10% shareholder requirement must be satisfied at both the time of purchase and the time of the sale. The person must have been a 10% shareholder before she purchased and before she sold.

The officer/director requirement is satisfied if the person was an officer and/or director both at the time of her purchase and of her sale of stock, or at the time of either her purchase or her sale of stock.

Second: How do you apply section 16(b)?

You are looking for section 16(b) profits, which are different from real world profits. In the real world, you make a profit when you buy something and then later sell it at a higher price. First you buy, then you sell for more.

Under section 16(b), you ignore the order in which the transactions occurred. There is a section 16(b) profit if purchase is followed by a sale at higher price, or if a sale is followed by a purchase at a lower price.

To illustrate, on January 10, D, a director of a 34 Act public company, buys 100 shares of his corporation's stock for $10 a share. On February 2, D sells 70 shares of the stock for $8 a share. On March 3, D buys 50 shares of the stock for $5 a share. On April 1, D sells 80 shares for $1 a share.

Under these facts, there is a $150 section 16(b) profit. A 50 share purchase for $5 a share occurred within 6 months of the sale of 50+ shares for $8 so the profit is computed as 50 shares × $3 profit ($8-$5) per share.

Under section 16(b), you would ignore the January 10 purchase at $10 a share. There is no sale within 6 months of January for a higher price.

Similarly, under section 16(b), you would ignore the April 1 sale at $1 a share. There is no purchase within six months of April 1 for an amount less than $1 a share.

I understand that if you were to net out all of D's stock transactions during this period, that D lost money. You need to understand that whether a director actually profited from all of their "short-swing" trading is irrelevant.

Think of section 16(b) as a kind of match game in which you only match sales with purchases at a lower price. Makes no sense.[11] That is why your professor is likely to test section 16(b) if your class covered it.

---

[11] Makes no sense unless you remember that the purpose of section 16(b) is to deter insiders from speculating in their corporations stock. Your professor might have used the term "prophylactic rule."

Third: How does section 16(b) differ from Rule 10b-5?

Let me count the ways.

First, a Rule 10b-5 recovery in a private action goes to the injured buying or selling shareholders. A section 16(b) recovery goes to the corporation whose stock was bought and sold in the six-month period.

Second, section 16(b) only applies if the stock transactions involved stock in a public company registered under the 34 Act. Rule 10b-5 is not so limited.

Third, section 16(b) only applies if the person engaged in the stock transactions is an officer, director, or 10% shareholder of that public corporation. Again, Rule 10b-5 is not limited.

Fourth, Rule 10b-5 only applies to defendants who do tacky things—make false statement or buy or sell stock relying on material inside information. Section 16(b) imposes strict liability on people—no need to prove that defendant did something wrong.

CHAPTER 24

What You Need to Know About Mergers and Acquisitions for a Basic Business Associations/ Organizations Course

Most law schools have an advanced corporations course called Mergers and Acquisitions. Nonetheless, most business associations/ organizations casebooks have materials on mergers and acquisitions, and some professors cover that stuff. If your professor is one of that "some," then there are seven things you need to know about mergers and acquisitions:

1. What is a merger?
2. What are the legal effects of a merger?
3. Who has to approve a merger?
4. What if a shareholder is unhappy about a merger?
5. How does a corporation's selling all (or substantially all) of its assets to another corporation differ from that corporation's merging into another corporation?

6. What is the de facto merger doctrine?
7. How are tender offers different from mergers or sales of assets?

1. What Is a Merger?

In a merger, two or more business entities combine into one business entity. For example, Acme Corp. merges into Baker Corp.

In this example, Acme Corp. would be referred as the "disappearing corporation" because it would, in fact and in law, disappear. Baker Corp. would be referred to as the "surviving corporation."

2. What Are the Legal Effects of a Merger?

MBCA section 11.07(a)(2) is typical of corporate codes in providing that "[w]hen a merger becomes effective . . . the separate existence of every corporation . . . that is merged into the survivor cease(s)."

It is not only the disappearing corporation's "existence" that is merged into the survivor, but also the disappearing corporation's assets and liabilities. When Acme Corp. merges into Baker Corp., all assets of Acme Corp. and all assets of Baker Corp. become assets of Baker Corp. And, all creditors of Acme Corp. and all creditors of Baker Corp. become creditors of Baker Corp.

Generally, the shareholders of the disappearing corporation give up their stock in the disappearing corporation and get stock in the surviving corporation. In such a stock for stock merger the shareholders of the disappearing Acme Corp. become shareholders of Baker Corp. The shareholders of Baker Corp., of course, remain shareholders of Baker Corp.

Another possibility is that the shareholders of the disappearing corporation receive cash instead of stock. In such a cash for stock merger (a/k/a a "cash out merger"), the shareholders of the disappearing Acme Corp. receive cash.

3. Who Has to Approve a Merger?

First, executives of the two corporations negotiate a merger agreement.

Then, the boards of directors of both of the merging companies must approve the merger. If Acme Corp. is merging into Baker Corp., the Acme Corp. board of directors and the Baker Corp. board of directors both must agree on a plan of merger.

Generally, the plan of merger must also be approved by the requisite majorities of the shareholders of both the disappearing and the surviving corporation. Under both the Delaware General Corporation Statute and the MBCA, an affirmative vote of the shareholders of the surviving corporation is not required if the number of outstanding voting shares of the surviving corporation after the combination is not increased by more than 20% from the number of outstanding voting shares before the combination.

4. What if a Shareholder Is Unhappy with the Proposed Plan of Merger?

You should already know three of the four things that a shareholder who is unhappy with a proposed merger can do.

First, you know that shareholders who are unhappy with the proposed merger can sell their shares.

Second, you know that shareholders who are unhappy with the proposed merger can vote against it.

Third, you know that (i) mergers also require decisions by the board of directors, and (ii) a shareholder who is unhappy with a decision of the board of directors can claim that the directors approving the merger breached their duty of care or duty of loyalty, if the facts support such a claim.

Watch for a merger agreement in which (i) the shareholders of the disappearing corporation receive cash and (ii) the majority shareholder of the disappearing corporation is also the owner of the surviving corporation. Such a merger is called a "freeze out merger" because the minority shareholder is forced out, i.e., "frozen out." When you see such a fact pattern in an exam question you are seeing an interested director transaction and your professor needs to see your application of the entire fairness doctrine discussed supra at page 132 et seq.

Fourth, and most important, you need to know about dissenting shareholders' appraisal rights. The phrase "appraisal rights" is incomplete and maybe even misleading. Shareholders who oppose a merger and comply with the detailed statutory requirements in Delaware General Corporation Statute section 262 (or MBCA Chapter 13 or whatever the relevant state corporation statute is) have more than the right to have their shares appraised or valued. Rather, a shareholder who properly assert their dissenting shareholder's right of appraisal can compel the corporation to pay them in cash the fair value of their shares as determined by a judicial appraisal process.

To illustrate, S is a 10% shareholder of Acme Corp., which merges into Baker Corp. The effect of the merger, of course, is that Acme Corp. and its shares both cease to exist. Assume that the merger agreement values Acme Corp. at $3,000,000 and so provides that Acme Corp. shareholders will receive consideration that has a value of $3,000,000. This consideration can be Baker Corp. stock or other property or cash. As a 10% shareholder of Acme Corp., S would receive 10% of that consideration, i.e. consideration with a value of $300,000.

Assume next that S instead properly asserts their dissenting shareholder's right of appraisal, and the court decides that the fair value of Acme Corp. is $5,000,000, and not $3,000,000. S, as a dissenting shareholder who owns 10% of the outstanding stock of Acme Corp. and seeks appraisal, has a right to $500,000 (10% of $5,000,000) in cash not $300,000 (10% of the $3,000,000 of total consideration actually received by Acme Corp).

Not all mergers trigger appraisal rights. Under the Delaware General Corporate Law section 262(b), appraisal rights are not available for shareholders of corporations whose stock is listed on a national securities exchange or which has more than 2,000 record shareholders. The MBCA and most states have similar provisions.

This statutory exclusion of appraisal rights makes sense. If a corporation's stock is publicly traded or if the corporation has a large number of shareholders, shareholders unhappy with a plan of merger have a market for their shares. They do not need an appraisal remedy, they can sell their shares.

State corporate statutes further limit the availability of appraisal. Shareholder must send notice to the corporation of their intent to exercise appraisal rights before the shareholder vote. Then, of course, the shareholder must later abstain or vote against the merger. Finally, if the merger is approved, the shareholder must timely tender their stock to the corporation and make a written demand for appraisal.

If the dissenting shareholder satisfies these requirements, then the court must determine the fair value of her shares. Corporate statutes provide little guidance as to how courts should determine fair value. According to *Weinberger v. UOP, Inc.*, a leading Delaware decision, courts can use any valuation technique considered acceptable in the financial community.

5. How Does a Corporation's Selling All (or Substantially All) of Its Assets to Another Corporation Differ from That Corporation's Merging into Another Corporation?

What if Acme Corp. sold all of its assets to Baker Corp. for Baker Corp. stock or for cash, instead of Acme Corp.'s merging into Baker Corp.? How is this sale of all assets similar to and different from a merger?

The two transactions are similar in that an end result of both is that Baker Corp. still exists. And, another end result of both is that Baker Corp. will own all assets that formerly belonged to Acme Corp. Finally, Acme Corp.'s sale of all of its assets to Baker Corp., like Acme Corp's merger into Baker Corp., would have to be approved by the board of directors of both corporations.

Now here are three, exam-important differences between a merger of Acme Corp. into Baker Corp. and Acme Corp.'s sale of all of its assets to Baker Corp.

5.1. Continued Existence of Acme Corp.

Remember that in "merger talk," Acme Corp. is called the "disappearing corporation" because Acme Corp. disappears when the merger is completed. Acme Corp.'s sale of all of its assets to Baker Corp. does not end Acme Corp.'s existence. Instead, Acme Corp.'s sale of all of its assets to Baker Corp. simply changes Acme Corp.'s assets from what it once owned, but has now sold to Baker Corp., to the proceeds from that sale.

While Acme Corp.'s sale of all of its assets to Baker Corp. does not automatically end Acme's Corp.'s existence, the existence of a corporation that sells all of its assets commonly ends shortly after the sale. The selling corporation often follows up the sale of all of its assets with dissolution (legal process of ending the corporation's existence) and liquidation (distribution of the sale proceeds first to the corporation's creditors and then to its shareholders).

5.2. Rights of Acme Corp.'s Creditors

After Acme Corp.'s merger into Baker Corp., Acme Corp.'s creditors become creditors of Baker Corp. After Acme Corp.'s sale of its assets to Baker Corp., Acme Corp.'s creditors remain creditors of Acme Corp.

This should make sense—in theory. After the sale of its assets to Baker Corp., Acme Corp. has the sale proceeds. In theory, those sale proceeds should have the same market value as the Acme Corp. assets that have been sold. Thus, in theory, Acme Corp.'s creditors have not been adversely affected by Acme Corp.'s sale of all of its assets.

5.3. Rights of Shareholders

In a merger, the shareholders of the disappearing corporation and the shareholders of surviving corporation have the same rights. Both have the right to vote on the merger; both have the same appraisal rights.

In a sale of assets, the shareholders of the selling corporation have a right to vote on the transaction and have appraisal rights. The shareholders of the buying corporation, however, have neither the right to vote on the transaction nor appraisal rights.

To review, Acme Corp.'s sale of all of its assets to Baker Corp. would have to be approved by (1) the board of directors of both Acme Corp. and Baker Corp. and (2) the shareholders of Acme Corp. The shareholders of Acme Corp. would have appraisal rights. The shareholders of Baker Corp., would not have a right to vote on Baker Corp.'s purchase of Acme Corp.'s assets and would not have appraisal rights unless the Baker Corp. shareholders are able to convince the court to apply the "de facto merger doctrine."

6. What Is the De Facto Merger Concept?

De facto merger is a creation of case law based on the "sound-good" concept that like things should be treated alike, that substance should be elevated over form. In some states, shareholders of a corporation that has bought all of the assets of another corporation have successfully invoked the de facto merger doctrine to gain appraisal rights.

Assume, for example, that Baker Corp. buys all of the assets of Acme Corp. As a result of the deal structure, Baker Corp.'s shareholders will not be entitled to vote and will not have appraisal rights. Unhappy Baker Corp. shareholders argue that the sale of assets is a de facto merger. If the court agrees, then the court will ignore the form of the transaction and grant Baker Corp. shareholders the right to vote and to appraisal.

The Delaware Supreme Court in *Hariton v. Aero Electronics*, rejected a shareholder's efforts to re-characterize a sale of assets as a de facto merger. *Hariton* elevated form over substance because that is what the Delaware legislature had done by providing different ways of accomplishing an acquisition with different consequences.

The de facto merger doctrine has also been invoked by creditors of the selling corporation in products liability cases and CERCLA cases brought against the buying corporation long after the dissolution of the selling corporation. Remember the successor liability cases you studied in torts? It is unlikely that you will need to remember those cases for your exam unless your BA/BO professor also teaches torts.

7. How Is a Tender Offer Different from a Merger or Asset Sale?

Both mergers and asset sales are forms of acquisition that require approval of the boards of directors of all affected corporations: the board of directors of both the surviving and disappearing corporation in a merger, the board of directors of both the buying and selling corporation in an asset sale. Often, the board of directors of the disappearing corporation will oppose a merger, or the board of directors of the selling corporations will oppose a sale. That opposition may be based on the substance (or lack of substance) of the transaction. More cynically, that opposition may be based on inside directors wanting to keep their well-paying jobs as corporate officers.

The tender offer is a form of acquisition that does not require the approval of the board of directors of the acquired corporation (a/k/a the "target corporation"). A tender offer is an offer made by the bidder directly to the shareholders of the target corporation to purchase their shares. The usual purpose of a tender offer is to acquire a sufficient number of shares of the target corporation to replace the target's present board of directors with directors more acceptable to the bidder.

A typical tender offer has the following characteristics:

- the target company is a public corporation that is a registered corporation;
- the offer is made at a fixed price which is at a premium above the prevailing market price;
- the offer is open for a limited period of time;

- the offer is contingent on shareholders' tendering some minimum number and/or maximum number of shares that the bidder will buy;
- the offer is communicated to all shareholders of the target corporation by means of newspaper advertisements and a general mailing.

If, as is usually the case, the tender offer is opposed by the board of directors of the target corporation, then the tender offer is referred to as a "hostile takeover." Actions taken by the board of directors of a target corporation to prevent a hostile takeover have such colorful names as "Pac Man," "poison pill," and "shark repellent" and are covered in a Merger and Acquisition course.

If the target corporation in a tender offer is a registered corporation, then the tender offer is regulated by the 34 Act. These regulations are covered in both Merger and Acquisitions courses and Securities Regulations courses.

PART 4

Limited Partnership

CHAPTER 25

What You Need to Know About Limited Partnerships

In considering what business structure to use for their horse feathers business, Groucho, Chico, and Harpo of course want "the best of both worlds." They want a business structure that provides both the favorable tax treatment of a partnership and the protection from personal liability of a corporation.

For most of the 20th century, the limited partnership was the business structure chosen by the Grouchos, Chicos, and Harpos of the world (and also by people with more common names) who wanted both the favorable tax treatment of a partnership and the protection from personal liability of a corporation.

For the last twenty-five years or so, limited liability companies, ("LLCs") not limited partnerships, have been their choice. Nonetheless, we need to understand what limited partnerships are and how they work because:

- most hedge funds are limited partnerships;

- many entertainment, oil and gas and real estate investment opportunities are limited partnerships; and
- there is a lot of similarity between limited partnership law and limited liability company law.

If your BA/BO class covered limited partnerships in more than one class meeting, here are the eight things that you need to know:

1. What is a limited partnership?
2. What is limited partnership law?
3. What are the legal problems involved in starting a business as a limited partnership?
4. Who makes the decisions for a limited partnership?
5. Who is liable for the debts of a limited partnership?
6. What are the duties of partners and limited partners to the partnership and other partners?
7. What can the owners of a limited partnership transfer?
8. How are limited liability partnerships different from limited partnerships?

1. What Is a Limited Partnership?

A limited partnership is a form of business structure that is similar to, but in some important respects different from, a partnership. Like a partnership, a limited partnership does not pay income tax on its earnings. And like a partnership, a limited partnership has partners.

Unlike a partnership, a limited partnership has two kinds of partners—(1) "regular, plain old vanilla partners" and (2) "limited partners." In a limited partnership, any "regular, plain old vanilla partner" has management rights and liability exposure for the partnership's debts that are similar to the management rights and liability exposure of "regular, plain old vanilla partners" in the "regular, plain old vanilla partnerships" we studied in Chapters 4-10.

[As you may recall, I did not use the adjectival phrase "regular, plain, old vanilla" in describing partners and partnerships in Chapters 4-10. And courts and other law professors do not use that phrase. Instead, they, and hereafter, I, describe such partners as "general partners" and describe the kind of partnerships we studied in Chapters 4-10 as "general partnerships" or simply "partnerships."]

In addition to one or more general partners who have the same legal rights and responsibilities as the partners in a general partnership, a limited partnership also has limited partners. A limited partnership usually has only one general partner; a limited partnership usually has multiple limited partners.

Unlike general partners, a limited partner does not have personal liability for the limited partnership's debts. The most a limited partner can lose from their investment in a limited partnership is their investment.

2. What Is Limited Partnership Law?

Every state has a limited partnership statute. Most are based on a uniform act. What complicates things is that there have been four uniform acts.

The original Uniform Limited Partnership Act (ULPA) was promulgated in 1916. A Revised Uniform Limited Partnership Act (RULPA) was promulgated in 1976 and further significant amendments were made in 1985. As if that were not enough, in 2001, a new version of RULPA was promulgated.

Most states, including Delaware, still have a limited partnership statute based on the 1985 RULPA. Most casebooks (and so this book) look primarily to the Delaware limited partnership statute. No matter what limited partnership statute applies, it is clear universally that a limited partnership is an entity.

It is also clear that a limited partnership is subject to federal securities laws such as Rule 10b-5 and state securities laws. A limited partnership interest—the name cleverly used to describe the ownership interest in limited partnership—is treated as a "security" by the federal and state securities laws, including Rule 10b-5. This makes sense because, as we will see repeatedly in this chapter, a limited partner in a limited partnership is like a shareholder in a corporation in that limited partners like shareholders are essentially passive investors in a business.

3. What Are the Legal Problems in Starting a Business as a Limited Partnership?

Unlike general partnerships (but like corporations), limited partnerships do not come into existence until there has been a public filing, usually with the secretary of state of the state of organization. That document is generally called a Certificate of Limited Partnership.

The two exam-important requirements for certificates of limited partnership are (1) the name of the business, which must include the term "limited partnership," or some abbreviation thereof—e.g., Horse Feathers, LP, and (2) the name and address of all general partners.

Even if the Certificate of Limited Partnership meets the requirements of the state's limited partnership law, that document alone will not meet the requirements of the business and its owners.

The more important document for limited partnerships is the limited partnership agreement.

Although RULPA does not require that there be a written limited partnership agreement, almost all limited partnerships have detailed written agreements. These partnership agreements define the relative roles of the limited partners and the general partner and largely supplant the limited partnership statute as the place to look for answers in resolving disputes between the limited partnership and partners and disputes among partners.

Recall that limited partnership statutes require that:

- a limited partnership must have at least one general partner;
- this general partner, unlike the limited partners, is liable for the debts of the partnership; and
- the name and the address of the general partner must be set out in the Certificate of Limited Partnership, which is filed in public records.

The limited partnership statutes do not, however, require that the general partner be a natural, flesh-and-blood person. The general partner can be a corporation.

This means that Groucho, Chico, and Harpo can set up a limited partnership in which none of them is the general partner, i.e., none of them is personally liable for the debts of the partnership. If Groucho, Chico, and Harpo want to structure their horse feathers business as a limited partnership and want to avoid personal liability, they take two simple steps: (1) organize a corporation, Horse Feathers, Inc., and (2) organize a limited partnership, Horse Feathers, Limited Partnership, with Horse Feathers, Inc. as the only general partner and each of them as limited partners. Then they use the limited partnership, Horse Feathers Limited Partnership, to own and operate the business.

Although Horse Feathers Inc. will now, as general partner, be "personally liable" for the limited partnership's liabilities, the owners of the corporation will not be. The corporate form protects Groucho, Chico, and Harpo from personal liability.

4. Who Makes Decisions for the Limited Partnership?

Unless the limited partnership agreement otherwise provides, the general partner makes the decisions for the limited partnership. Typically, the limited partners are merely passive investors. Limited partners often have less of a role in a limited partnership's decision making than shareholders have in a corporation's decision making.

In limited partnerships, the relationship between general and limited partners is usually only financial. Limited partners tend to be investors who are putting money into a business run by a business entity general partner that is run by people whom they do not know personally. On the other hand, relationships between partners of general partnerships are usually part financial and part personal, with a division of control between the partners.

5. Who Is Liable for the Debts of a Limited Partnership?

There is a four-part answer to the question who is liable for the debts of a limited partnership. First part, the limited partnership is an entity and so it is liable for its own debts. Second part, the general partners are jointly and severally liable for the debts of the limited partnership. (Remember, limited partnership statutes treat the general partners of a limited partnership the same way that partnership statutes treat partners.) Third part, the limited partners of a limited partnership are generally not liable for the debts of a limited partnership. (Remember, limited partners, like shareholders, are generally passive investors, and so, like shareholders, are not personally liable for the business's debts.) Fourth part, the limited partners can be liable for the debts of the of the limited partnership if . . . .

This fourth part of the answer to the question "who is liable for the debts of a limited partnership" is the most "exam-important" part. What you are most likely to see on your exam are facts that suggest that a limited partner is something more than a passive investor—facts that suggest that perhaps that limited partner should be personally liable for the debts of the limited partnership.

Historically, there has been a correlation between whether a limited partner is active in making decisions for the limited partnership and whether the limited partner is personally liable to the creditors of the limited partnership. Increasingly, limited partnership statutes have decreased the possible liability of limited partners for debts of the limited partnership.

Under RULPA, for example, a limited partner is personally liable for the debts of the limited partnership only if they "participate[s] in the control of the business but also their conduct causes the creditor to believe she was a general partner." Moreover, the statute sets out "safe harbors," i.e., things that a limited partner can do without participating "in the control of the business," such as:

- voting on the admission or removal of a general partner;
- voting on the limited partnership's selling assets or incurring debt; and
- serving as a director or officer of the corporate general partner.

6. What Are the Duties of Partners and Limited Partners to the Limited Partnership?

Now let's consider the question of who is liable to the limited partnership because their wrongful acts or inaction has damaged the limited partnership. Another four-point answer:

First part, the limited partner has no such liability exposure. The limited partner, like a shareholder, is a passive investor and so, like a shareholder, owes no legal duties to the business entity.

Second part, the general partner of a limited partnership does have liability exposure to the limited partnership. The general partner of a limited partnership has the same duty of care and duty of loyalty as the general partner of a partnership, and if she breaches that duty she is liable, except as provided below.

Third part, under the Delaware limited partnership statute, the limited partnership agreement can eliminate the general partner's duty of care. Remember there is a comparable provision in the Delaware General Corporation Law which permits a corporation's certificate to eliminate the directors' duty of care. In addition, a Delaware limited partnership agreement can also eliminate the general partner's duty of loyalty but "may not eliminate the implied contractual covenant of good faith and fair dealing."

Fourth part, there is dicta in *In re USACafes, L.P. Litigation*, a Delaware trial court case, that the director of a corporate general partner owes a duty of care and duty of loyalty not only to the corporate general partner but also to the limited partnership. So, if Groucho is a director of Horse Feathers, Inc., which is the general partner of Horse Feathers Limited Partnership, then Groucho owes a duty of care and a duty of loyalty to both Horse Feathers, Inc. and Horse Feathers Limited Partnership. No case has yet expressly addressed the obvious question of what Groucho does when the interests of Horse Feathers, Inc. and Horse Feathers Limited Partnership do not coincide.

7. What Can the Owners of a Limited Partnership Sell?

Remember the legal obstacles to a partner's sale of her equity interest in the partnership? To review, under RUPA, partners in a general partnership can only sell their "transferable interests", i.e., their financial rights but not their management rights. On the other hand, shareholders can sell their shares, i.e., their "management (voting) rights" as well as their financial rights.

It is understandable that a general partner in a limited partnership should be under the same statutory constraints as a general partner in a partnership. A general partner in a limited partnership, like a general partner in a partnership, makes decisions that impact the other owners of the business.

If Groucho is the general partner of Horse Feathers Limited Partnership, he makes decisions that impact the limited partners Chico and Harpo. General partner Groucho should not be able to sell that decision making power to Zeppo. And so, limited partnership statutes impose the same transfer constraints on the general partner in a limited partnership as RUPA imposes on the partners in a partnership.

What is harder to understand is why limited partnership statutes impose the same sale constraint on the limited partners of a limited partnership. Limited partners do not make decisions that impact the other owners of the business.

If limited partner Chico sells his interest in Horse Feathers, LP to Gummo, that would have no possible effect on the other owners of Horse Feathers, LP. Nonetheless, limited partnership statutes place the same constraint on transfers by limited partners as on transfers by general partners. Limited partners like Chico can only sell their "transferable interests", i.e., their financial interests.

8. What Are the Differences Between a Limited Partnership and a Limited Liability Partnership?

We have been studying the limited partnership, a business entity governed by state limited partnership statutes, in which:

- at least one partner is a general partner;
- other partners are limited partners;
- the general partner is personally liable to the limited partnership's creditors for the limited partnership's debts; and
- the limited partners are not generally liable to the limited partnership's creditors for the limited partnership's debt.

Now we need to learn about the limited liability partnership (LLP), a business entity governed by state partnership statutes, in which:

- all partners are general partners and
- all the general partners are protected from liability to creditors of the limited liability partnership.

LLPs were invented by the Texas legislature to protect accountants and lawyers in big firms structured as general partnerships from personal liability for malpractice by their partners. Other states followed Texas' lead. All states now have LLP statutory provisions.

State LLP statutory provisions vary considerably from state to state. In some states, the LLP can be used only by partnerships practicing a profession and not by general business partnerships. In some states, partners in an LLP are protected only from liability for negligence claims, and thus remain vicariously liable for the limited partnership debts arising from contracts and from the intentional torts of other partners.

In all states, LLPs must file a certificate with the designated state official that includes the firm's name, which must contain the words "limited liability partnership" or the "LLP" abbreviation, and state that the business is being operated as a limited liability partnership. In addition, some states require an LLP to maintain a specified amount of liability insurance or provide a pool of funds for the satisfaction of judgments against the LLP.

Again, notwithstanding the name "limited liability partnership," an LLP is not a limited partnership. An LLP is a special form of general partnership in which the general partners have no liability for the LLP's debts.

PART 5

Limited Liability Companies

CHAPTER 26

What You Need to Know About Limited Liability Companies

Most new businesses use the limited liability company structure. When Walter and Skyler got into the car wash business, their lawyer Saul probably formed a limited liability company.

A limited liability company is called an "LLC." The owners of an LLC such as Walter and Skyler are called "members."

An LLC is in some respects like a partnership and in other respects like a corporation. And like a limited partnership, an LLC offers its members both (i) protection from liability for the business's debts similar to the liability protection of shareholders of a corporation, and (ii) the same pass-through income tax treatment as a partnership.

1 If LLCs Are So Important, Why Is the Part of the Book on LLCs So Short?

The reasons that the LLC unit of this book is so short are the same as the reasons that your professor spent so few classes on LLCs. First, the answers to most LLC questions turn on the interpretation of the provisions of a contract generally referred to as the operating agreement, not LLC statutes or case law. Second, LLC statutes vary widely from state to state. Some borrow more from corporate laws; others borrow more from partnership law. Third, the questions that arise in forming, operating, growing, and ending a business structured as an LLC are similar to the partnership and corporation questions, and the legal concepts triggered by the questions are similar to the legal concepts already covered in the partnership, corporations, and limited partnership chapters of this book.

2. What Law Governs LLCs?

The LLC is a relatively new business structure in the United States. Its origins trace to a statute enacted in Wyoming in 1978. Use of LLCs became widespread only after 1997 changes in the tax law clarified that LLCs would receive the same single tax treatment as partnerships.

Each state now has a statute authorizing the creation of LLCs. These statutes typically borrow both from partnership law and corporation law.

LLC statutes vary greatly from state to state. There is far more variety in state LLC laws than we find in the corporation or partnership laws of the various states. The National Conference of Commissioners on Uniform State Law issued a Uniform Limited Liability Company Act (ULLCA) in 1996 and issued a substantially revised version (RULLCA) in 2006. Neither has been widely adopted.

What is most important about LLC statutes is how unimportant the statutes are. In the main, LLC problems are answered by contract provisions rather than the provisions of the LLC statute. LLC statutes set out primarily "default rules", i.e., rules that apply only if there is no agreement to the contrary.

3. What Are the Legal Steps in Starting an LLC?

Like corporations and limited partnerships, LLCs do not exist until a formal filing with the state. Some state law uses the term "certificate of formation" and others use the term "articles of organization" to describe the document that must be filed to create an LLC.

That document typically contains very little information about the company. Obviously, the document must include the name of the LLC. And, that name must include the words "limited liability company" or the abbreviation "LLC."

A limited liability company's most important document is the "Operating Agreement." The operating agreement is not a public document, i.e., it is not filed. State limited liability company statutes do not even require that there be an operating agreement.

As the term "operating agreement" suggests, an operating agreement governs how the limited liability company operates. In resolving disputes over the operation of a limited liability company, courts look first to the operating agreement.

And, so, as you answer exam questions involving the operation of a limited liability company, look first for facts about operating agreement provisions. LLC laws give maximum effect to operating agreements. Again, most LLC statute provisions are "default rules," i.e., applicable only if the LLC's operating agreement does not otherwise provide.

4. Who Makes Decisions for a Business Structured as an LLC?

The owners of an LLC can select the form of management. Every state's LLC statute affords the owners (members) the option of electing to manage the business themselves—"member-managed company"—or have managers—"manager-managed company"—or some combination of member-managed and manager-managed.

The decision-making authority of the members of a member-managed company is much like that of the partners in a general partnership. And the decision-making authority of the managers of a manager-managed company is much like a corporation with a board of directors, professional managers, and separation of ownership and management.

In a member-managed company, the operating agreement will answer such questions as: (1) how to determine how many votes each member has and (2) how to determine what matters require more than majority vote. In a manager-managed company, the operating agreement will answer questions such as: (1) how members elect and remove managers and (2) what matters require members vote.

5. Who Is Liable for an LLC's Debts?

An LLC is an entity. An LLC can incur debts from the actions and inactions of its managers or its agents.

State statutes differ greatly as to who is an agent for a limited liability company. In Delaware, the default rule is that both managers and members are agents; ULLCA provides that members are agents if the LLC is member-managed but only managers are agents if the LLC is manager-managed; and RULLCA provides that members are not agents "solely by reason of being a member."

More important, all LLC statutes provide that managers and members of an LLC are not liable to the company's creditors. These statutes do not distinguish the personal liability of members in member-managed LLCs from the personal liability of members in manager-managed LLCs. The managers and members are simply not liable for the company's debts.

Recall that, under principles of corporation law, the limited liability of a shareholder of a corporation is limited by the concept of piercing the corporate veil. Corporation statutes do not provide for piercing the corporate veil. It is a case law common concept.

Similarly, the limited liability of a member of an LLC is limited by piercing the veil. Most LLC statutes do not provide for piercing the veil. Again, piercing the veil law comes from case law.

As with the corporate law cases, the LLC piercing cases simply provide a list of factors to be considered. The biggest difference between corporate piercing cases and LLC piercing cases is that the LLC cases do not emphasize disregard of operational formalities to the extent that the corporate cases do.

6. Who Owes Fiduciary Duties to an LLC?

Absent a contrary provision in the operating agreement, "traditional" fiduciary duties are owed by managers in a manager-managed LLC, and members in a member-managed LLC, but not by members in a manager-managed LLC. These fiduciary duties normally include duties of loyalty and care similar to those found in partnerships and corporations.

What you need to watch for in an exam fact pattern, in which LLC managers or members are doing "tacky things," is information about the operating agreement. Notice the introductory phrase "Absent a contrary provision in the operating agreement." The Delaware LLC statute, like the Delaware limited partnership act, provides that the operating agreement can eliminate managers' duty of care and duty of loyalty but not the "implied contractual covenant of good faith and fair dealing."

7. What Can the Owners of an LLC Sell?

The most important limitation on an LLC member's making money by selling their interest for more than they paid for it is imposed by the market, not by the legislature, the courts, or even the operating agreement. It is usually difficult to find a buyer for a minority interest in a small business, or even a minority interest in large business, that has relatively few owners.

Even if a member of a limited liability company is able to find a buyer for their interest, a member's ability to sell may be limited by statute, or by the operating agreement, or by both. Recall what you learned about a partner's sale of their "transferable" interest. Unlike a shareholder, but like a partner, an LLC member is barred by statute from selling full ownership interest to an outsider. LLC statutes, like partnership statutes and limited partnership statutes, provide that an LLC member can sell their financial rights but not their management rights. Even in manager-managed LLCs where a member's management rights are often less than a shareholder's management rights.

8. What Do You Need to Know About Dissociation by an LLC Member?

Because of the market constraints and legal restrictions on a members' sale of their ownership interest in a limited liability company to an outsider, the question of whether members of an LLC can compel the company to purchase their ownership interest is often important.

Recall a partner's power to compel the partnership to purchase her ownership interest by invoking the RUPA concept of dissociation. I hope that you don't recall a shareholder's power to compel the corporation to purchase her shares by invoking the concept of dissociation. There is no corporate law equivalent of dissociation.

And, in some states, there is no limited liability equivalent of dissociation. For example, the Delaware LLC statute does not even use the term "dissociation." Instead, the Delaware LLC statute provides that a member may not resign from an LLC prior to dissolution unless an LLC agreement otherwise provides. In other states, a member's dissociation does not obligate the LLC to buy the dissociating member's interest unless the LLC agreement otherwise provides.

The last two sentences provide an appropriate reminder that even though most new business associations are limited liability companies you should spend most of your exam review time on corporations. First, most LLC questions are answered by LLC agreements, not statutes. Second, those LLC questions not answered by LLC agreements are answered differently by the very different LLC state statutes.

Last Words

Your professor gets the "last word."

Your professor might have different ideas from mine as to what is important. Your professor might even have some different ideas from mine as to what the law is.

Clearly, I am right and your professor is wrong. And clearly, that is not what is important.

What is important is that your professor is the one who grades your exam. So, your professor has the last word (unless you want to have the last word by sending me an email when you get that "A" grade in your business associations/organizations class).

David

depstein@richmond.edu